YOGA CRAZE IN THE LAST DAYS

ARE YOU TRADING YOUR TRUE DESTINY FOR A SPIRITUAL COUNTERFEIT?

DAVE WILLIAMS, D. MIN, D.D.

Award-winning, Best-selling Author

YOGA CRAZE IN THE LAST DAYS

Are You Trading Your True Destiny for a
Spiritual Counterfeit?
by Dave Williams

Yoga Craze in the Last Days
Copyright © 2019 by David R. Williams
ISBN: 9781629850696
Cover Design by: Aikaterini
Editor: Kathleen Manges

www.DaveWilliams.com

19 20 21 22 23 – 9 8 7 6 5 4 3 2 1

Printed in the United States of America

ACKNOWLEDGMENTS AND SPECIAL THANKS

Thank you to my editor, Kathleen Manges, who is the most detail-oriented person I've ever known. She is also an author in her own right.

I also want to thank all the former Yoga instructors who shared the truth about Yoga with me, including the "Christian" brands of Yoga.

Also, I'm also grateful for the teachers, researchers. and apologists I've cited in this book, all of whom are committed to Jesus Christ and who love people enough to give them the unvarnished truth about pagan practices.

CONTENTS

FOREWORD

by Kirstin Baisch
Former Certified Yoga Instructor

You probably picked up this book because you're curious. Maybe you really want to know the truth about yoga, or the reality of its power to bring you into demonic, dark encounters. Or perhaps you grabbed this book because someone you love has begun their journey down the shadowy path of yoga, and you're praying that their eyes would be opened to the truth about the yoga deception.

As a former yoga teacher, I know first-hand about the dangers of this practice most believe is just an exercise. If you want to know the truth about the Yoga Craze you are seeing in the world today, and how it relates to the last days just before Christ returns, then you've picked up the right book. There is hope for anyone who is trapped in a satanic plot, and there is a way out. You will find it in this book, *Yoga Craze in the Last Days* by Dr. Dave Williams.

11

Is yoga more than just a physical exercise? Can I practice yoga if I'm a Christian? Can yoga be holy? Whether you're looking for answers to your questions, considering whether or not you should give yoga a try, or if you already practice it, you'll find the answers in this book and gain remarkable clarity on the true nature of yoga.

It's amazing how something with such deep ties to sorcery, like yoga, can be so strongly appealing. For me, I was hooked on yoga after my first class. I became a yoga disciple, totally sold out to the practice, sprinting deeper and deeper into its dark deception. I told everyone about yoga and was constantly encouraging people to try it. I went from innocently taking an exercise class to adopting a whole new lifestyle and culture. It seemed so harmless.

Honestly, I wish I had read a godly book like *Yoga Craze in the Last Days* back then. It may have saved me from the many demonic arrows that penetrated my life as a result of innocently, but mistakenly, launching headlong into the occult practice of yoga.

While I was in India receiving further yoga training, the demons I had attracted over the years began to manifest themselves in my life. There were multiple instances that shook my spirit to the core and caused me to wake up to the real invisible, sinister forces of darkness behind the practice of yoga.

After encountering these frightening demonic manifestations, God, in His mercy, began to speak to me very clearly. He showed me through a vision that the path of yoga would lead to death; a death very specifically surrounded by horrible flames. I learned later that my godly spirit-filled parents were back home interceding in prayer for me to return to the knowledge of the truth, and make things right with God. Their prayers were working.

I knew I had to leave the yoga practice. After years of practicing and hundreds of hours of devoting myself to yoga, I walked away. I left without saying a word to anyone. The spiritual and cultural tie that enslaved me was so strong I couldn't bear to say goodbye, although I knew I must leave.

Tears streamed down my face as the Lord poured out His love on me. I found out that even though I had practiced what the Bible said was forbidden, Jesus never stopped loving me. He gently nudged my spirit and led me back to His heart.

Having walked through the precise deception Dave Williams writes about in *Yoga Craze in the Last Days*, I can attest to everything he shares to be correct.

Dave shines the truth and light of Christ on the darkness of yoga. Each statement is clearly and directly backed by Scripture. There is no confusion about it. Starting in Chapter One, he exposes the lie of "Christian Yoga."

Dave is 100% accurate when he writes, "There can be no such thing as Christian Yoga." Yoga can never be holy or "Christianized."

Since coming back to Christ and being set free from the spirit behind yoga, I have seen the glory of God shine all about me.

I once questioned God in anger. Now I know the sound of His voice and the love He has for me. He has shown Himself to me through countless dreams, time in prayer, words from a friend, and in worship, to name a few ways.

He has given me wisdom and the ability to discern, and He has guided and counseled me. He has blessed me with an amazing husband, a huge family that loves me, a healthy body and mind!

He really has changed everything. I was truly ignorant to my sin. I was blinded and, like most who are deceived by yoga, I didn't believe that what I was doing could possibly be malignant or disastrous to my future. Yoga seemed like a healthy thing to do.

For six months after leaving the yoga practice, I faced a dreadful inner warfare as the dark demonic forces persisted in tugging on my spirit to return. In desperation, I cried out, "God, pull me closer. Take control Lord, I'm weak. I need you." And, like a miracle, He pulled me close, He clutched me in His arms, He lifted me up, He made me a brand-new person. He changed everything; something yoga couldn't do for me.

Jesus has now given me a brand-new beautiful life. I see His goodness clearly now, all around me. He has blessed me with an amazing husband and family, a beautiful home, a business doing what I love, and so much more!

I want for you and others to know Jesus the way I do. There are so many reasons; but mainly, I want for their lives to be transformed and renewed, to be lived with joy and freedom! I want you and those you love to experience the love of Jesus and the way He can transform your life. There is a fullness of life to be enjoyed. There is freedom. There is love. These things come from Jesus Christ alone.

Dave speaks to the eventual disaster that arises in the lives of those who practice yoga. I can speak to the reality of this as I myself experienced remarkable turmoil and disaster in my life while practicing yoga. An autoimmune disease attacked my body, relationships with those I love became seriously fractured, my mind was altered, and the beliefs and values I once held had completely changed.

The list is endless. As we know, the devil comes to kill, steal, and destroy (John 10:10). He is sneaky, like a serpent (which we were taught in yoga to be asleep at the base of the spine). This serpent, known as Satan, or "Kundalini," has found his way into destroying many lives through yoga.

In this book, you'll learn the tactics used by the devil to sneak into lives through yoga, regardless of the deceptive names yoga leaders use for their practices. You'll see "Yoga Med Centers," "Yoga Fitness Centers," "Yoga Health Centers," "Christian Yoga Studios," and other deceptive names, which disguise what yoga really is. As I read Dave's manuscript for *Yoga Craze in the Last Days*, I recognized the exact steps that led me into the trap and ensnarement.

I am pleased to write the Foreword for this well-researched book. Prepare to find gentle, non-condemning answers and astonishing truths you never knew before as you read Yoga Craze in the Last Days.

Kirstin Baisch
Former Certified Yoga Instructor

Kirstin Baisch is a former certified yoga teacher who now serves Jesus Christ. She lives in the heart of Michigan with her husband, Gavin, daughter Georgia, and their boxer-pit mix, Baby.

CHAPTER 1

YOGA CRAZE IN THE LAST DAYS

Read This First!

Dear children, keep away from anything that might take God's place in your hearts.
~ 1 John 5:21 NLT

Nearly 40 years ago Constance Cumby, in her book, *Hidden Dangers of the Rainbow*, warned the Church about the New Age concepts that were beginning to penetrate Christianity.[1] But did we pay attention? Many believers dismissed the warning, thinking she was just another alarmist or scaremonger.

Dr. Douglas Groothuis followed with his book, *Unmasking the New Age—Is There a New Religious Movement Trying to Transform Society?*[2] He presented evidence that the New Age was shifting out of the counterculture into the mainstream of society. Now, thirty-some years later, its occult effects are felt in nearly every aspect of life including medicine, politics, science, psychology and even religion.

THEY ARE SITTING IN YOUR CHURCH

New Agers teach a various blend of karma, chakras, yoga, higher consciousness, Christ consciousness, mindfulness (Eastern meditation), crystal powers, spirit channeling, and psychic powers. Today, naïve people that practice some of these identical concepts are sitting in our church pews spreading a counterfeit gospel to others. And typically, they don't know it.

Paul issued a stern message to the elders at Ephesus that warned about twisted teachers that would arise right from among the Church.

> **Acts 20:29-30 (MEV)**
> 29 For I know that after my departure, dreadful wolves will enter among you, not sparing the flock.
>
> 30 Even from among you men will arise speaking perverse things, to draw the disciples away after them.

And Peter warned believers:

> **1 Peter 5:8 (MEV)**
> Be sober and watchful, because your adversary the devil walks around as a roaring lion, seeking whom he may devour.

This book, *Yoga Craze in the Last Days*, heralds a solemn and ominous warning to those who are toying with yoga, *even as just an exercise.*

Why am I writing about yoga and why is this important to you and your own future?

The answer is simple. I have observed many Christians mistakenly getting involved in something they innocently think is a Christian exercise. I am writing this because my heart aches to bring them the truth about the practice of yoga, and show how it fits perfectly into a prophesied pattern in the last days.

An increasing number of Christians are unintentionally departing from the faith by unwittingly practicing the very things God hates.

I do not condemn those who practice yoga. I do, however, want to issue an honest, loving, and urgent warning about the severe consequences of engaging in this spiritually risky and deceptive system.

I am quite certain I will be criticized, mocked, and misunderstood. Whenever someone speaks for God's honor, typically he will be belittled in a sarcastic manner by those who think in a twisted way. It goes with the job-description of the discerner.

Jeremiah 6:17 (NLT)
I posted watchmen over you who said, 'Listen for the sound of the alarm.' But you replied, 'No! We won't pay attention!'

According to the *Springfield News-Sun*, when Pastor John Lindell passionately warned his congregation about the dangers of yoga, people immediately hurled insults, calling his sermon "ludicrous," "ignorant," and "divisive."[3]

Before you express your personal opinion, please just honestly read the research in this book and explore the 300+ references I have cited.

Isaiah, the prophet, saw what was coming to his people for their pagan practices and said, "Let me cry for my people as I watch them being destroyed." (Isaiah 22:4b NLT). I think I understand how the prophet felt.

I have listened to the heart-wrenching testimonies of those who, after time, suffered confusion, demonic oppression, and even physical maladies after delving into yoga. I rejoiced when they turned to the real Jesus Christ, not the "guru", but the Savior. Those who really did turn to Christ immediately began warning others of the dark, nefarious path on which others were embarking when they signed up for a yoga class.

My goal is to honor God by bringing the truth about yoga to America and the English-speaking world, and to reach the misguided souls who are practicing this ancient form of shamanism, sorcery, pantheism and self-worship.

Maybe you know someone who practices yoga and you've had a certain "feeling" about it you just cannot explain. That "feeling" is likely God's loving discernment, warning you about a hidden and potentially lethal danger.

With God's help, this book may deliver an eye-opening revelation to those dear souls who have been misled by the spiritually unqualified teachers and promoters of yoga.

The Christian Church, including Charismatics, Pentecostals, and Evangelicals, is exploding with occult practices that only a few years ago were characterized as spiritual counterfeits. Today we read about "Christian witches,"[4] "Christian Wicca,"[5] "Christian mediums,"[6] "Christian psychics"[7] and now "Christian Yoga."[8]

2 Timothy 4:3 (MEV)
For the time will come when people will not endure sound doctrine, but they will gather to themselves teachers in accordance with their own desires, having itching ears

Because it's currently taking the Church by storm, I'm focusing exclusively on yoga in this book. Do the ear-tickling "benefits" outweigh the spiritual consequences? Why does yoga wield such a mysterious, peculiar appeal?

What does God say? What do those who escaped from the yoga snare tell us? Are there undisclosed dangers and unexpected, dark after-effects? My goal is to answer these questions for you in *Yoga Craze in the Last Days*.

Repeatedly in this book, you will read, "Discernment is our lifeline."

We are unquestionably living in the day that was prophesied long ago when people would reject solid biblical doctrine and instead chase after unqualified teachers who embrace and espouse "doctrines of demons."[9]

Thank God for discerning Christians. My friend Jillian ordered a yoga workout video, but every time she tried to exercise with it, an uncanny spiritual sense enveloped her and gently said, "This is off limits for you." She now knows that "spiritual sense" was discernment from the Lord. She never practiced yoga again.

SOME WILL NOT READ THIS

Some will probably not finish reading this introduction. They'll toss away the book, then, they will brag to others, "I read a few paragraphs and tossed that book into the trash."

But, honestly, it's not an expression of sincere wisdom to refuse instruction from someone who cares about you.

Galatians 4:16-17 (TPT)
[16] Have I really become your enemy because I tell you the truth?

[17] Can't you see what these false teachers are doing? They want to win you over so you will side with them. They want you divided from me so you will follow only them. Would you call that integrity?

When I learned about the Christian Yoga brands that were popping up across America, I researched their teachers' books, videos, and blogs. I wanted to know what they were teaching. I even read Patañjali's *Yoga Sutras*, translated into English by a Harvard professor.[10] I was stunned to discover the clear threads of sorcery in Patañjali's writings, and wondered how followers of Jesus could participate in an ancient occult practice like this.

So, like Isaiah, I began to research and write.

Isaiah 30:8-10 (NLT)
Now go and write down these words. Write them in a book. They will stand until the end of time as a witness that these people are stubborn rebels who refuse to pay attention to the Lord's instructions. They tell the seers, "Stop seeing visions!" They tell the prophets, "Don't tell us what is right. Tell us nice things. Tell us lies."

MOVING AWAY FROM THE ONE TRUE GOD

I painfully discovered that yoga—any brand of yoga—actually makes you move away from the one true God of the

Bible and pulls you toward a counterfeit god, while deceiving you into believing you are "connecting" with the true God.

Faith is not faith unless it is firmly rooted in God's revealed Word and His promises. For example, you cannot say, "Adultery" is fine if you re-name it "holy adultery."

And you cannot take one-sixth of the Hindu doctrines, re-intention them for worship of Jesus, re-name them "holy," and practice them "in faith." That is not faith and that is not grace. Instead, it is disobedience and disgrace.

In my research, I learned that the physical postures in yoga are an intrinsic and vital part of a sorcery-ridden false religion that changes you mentally and spiritually.[11] That's the real purpose of yoga. It is not designed as a mere physical exercise, but to subtly refashion your mind to occult views.

What the repeated practice of yoga does is to push out the spirit of Jesus, replacing it with another spirit, regardless of the music playing in the background or on what or whom you are meditating.

Yoga was specifically fashioned to alter your mind to pagan and demonic mysticism. If you don't believe it, just listen to the scores of testimonies from precious souls like Corrina Craft, Jessica Smith, Kirstin Baisch, or Mike Shreve, who each have renounced the spirit behind yoga and returned to the real Jesus Christ of the Bible.

In essence, when we engage in yoga, we are committing adultery with pagan gods. Inescapably, deception and delusion will always follow.

I know this may sound outrageous to you because you probably think yoga is just a stretching and breathing exercise. That's why I ask you to please read this book, check my references, and then, make your decision.

I will show you in *Yoga Craze in the Last Days* that yoga is inseparably linked to the demonic realm. It *cannot* be disconnected from sorcery and divination. You *cannot* change yoga's nature by putting a Christian name tag on it and calling it "Christian" or "holy."

After years of researching this subject, talking with experienced individuals, listening to testimonies, and examining God's Word, I have come to believe that *yoga actually wields the preternatural power to separate you from Jesus* and open you and your family to treacherous demonic influences and spiritual attacks.

ANSWERS TO YOUR QUESTIONS ABOUT YOGA

With the Lord's help, I want to assist you in asking some serious, life-preserving questions about yoga. I have listed 94 of those questions here. Before reading *Yoga Craze in the Last Days,* see if you can answer these questions:

1. Do you believe yoga is just a stretching exercise?

2. Was yoga ever a biblically endorsed practice for Christians?

3. Are yoga poses honoring to demons?

4. Is yoga compatible with *genuine* Christianity?

5. Does yoga possess occult ties?

6. Why does disaster come to God's people?

7. Is 'Christian Yoga' different than Hindu-style Yoga?

8. Does yoga conjure up a 'Counterfeit Holy Spirit?'

9. Are there alternatives to Hindu-style Yoga?

10. What could possibly be wrong with meditating on God's Word, worshiping Jesus, listening to Christian music, and doing yoga poses at the same time?

11. What's the difference between "Encounters with the Holy Spirit" and "encounters with the kundalini spirit?"

12. Are there sincere people who practice "holy yoga?"

13. Is "Pre-Hindu" Yoga safe for Christians?

14. Does yoga cause you to trade your God-given destiny for a counterfeit?

15. Is yoga *really* good for you?

16. What are the origins of the Serpent Cult?

17. What does yoga have to do with the coming Antichrist in the last days?

18. Will "Vishnu" bring the "Age of Truth" to the Earth?

19. Is it possible to connect with a demonic entity in yoga and think it is God?

20. What is the reason for massive mental illness in America?

21. Can yoga alter your consciousness?

22. Is yoga a part of the end-time occult invasion?

23. Can yoga veil your true destiny and anointing?

24. What are five traits of professing Christians who practice yoga?

25. Does yoga carry and transmit a certain spirit?

26. Did God warn his people about mixing pagan practices into their faith?

27. Is yoga a certain type of Spiritualism or "spirit-ism?"

28. Can yoga actually disrupt or shipwreck a person's faith?

29. Is Hatha Yoga a springboard into deeper levels of deception?

30. Is yoga a religion or a science?

31. Is yoga a form of narcissism masquerading as humility?

32. How do Christian Yoga teachers justify their practices?

33. Is it really only the intention in yoga that matters?

34. How many sex scandals are there in yoga?

35. Did yoga begin as a sex cult?

36. Why do Christians join yoga groups today?

37. How does the devil seduce undiscerning believers?

38. Does yoga cause a loss of spiritual discernment?

39. Is the lotus pose a sexual/spiritual event?

40. Is there a connection between yoga and lust?

41. What is the dark side of yoga?

42. Who is the counterfeit Holy Spirit?

43. Can I bring demonic entities into my home after yoga class?

44. Is Heaven so bankrupt that you have to borrow from the devil?

45. What are the typical teaching phrases of *both* New Age and Christian Yoga instructors?

46. Is Christian Yoga a model based on theft?

47. What are some of the yoga slogans, half-truths and biblical misrepresentations?

48. Do Christian Yoga brands undermine the nature of Jesus Christ?

49. Did an exorcist really cast yoga demons out of professing Christians?

50. What is the prerequisite for the Holy Spirit to speak to you?

51. Which yoga teachers endorse "The Yoga Sutras of Patañjali?"

52. Is yoga really a part of the occult?

53. How can I recognize a subterfuge when I confront a deceived individual?

54. What are the five missteps into a fatal deception?

55. Is it true that yoga is not such a great exercise after all?

56. Are yoga-related injuries on the rise...including strokes?

57. Was yoga popular in Hitler's Third Reich?

58. Was there a yoga craze in Germany just before the Holocaust?

59. Was a yogi the mastermind behind the extermination camps?

60. Did the German people understand the demons they were summoning?

61. Did Germany experience a "collective awakening" from Hindu demons?

62. Why does yoga wield such a strong, weird attraction?

63. Is yoga the greatest fraud ever perpetrated against American women?

64. Does Christian-style Yoga attract a strong delusion?

65. Why does horrible blindness come over some professing believers?

66. Does yoga provide a progressive pathway into the occult?

67. Is Jesus your Guru? Are you worshiping the wrong Jesus?

68. What about the "OMS" and the "Chakras?"

69. Does Shiva, the "lord of yoga" demand the worship of his "lingam?"

70. Are you feasting on the polluted "Yoga Cake?"

71. Did early Church leaders deal with Hindu practices entering the Church?

72. Did St. Paul, himself, issue a serious warning about yoga?

73. Are yoga teachers actually Hindu missionaries?

74. Does yoga pervert faith and negatively affect the Church?

75. Is it true that yoga teachers are not licensed in U.S.A.?

76. Are the faith-brands of yoga teachers biblically accurate?

77. How is Syncretism distorting the truth and misleading many today?

78. Are unqualified teachers invading the Church?

79. Why do so many bite into the demonic bait?

80. Does yoga promote propaganda, half-truths, and illusory truth?

81. Does the truth matter to the yoga teachers?

82. Does yoga strip your spiritual defenses?

83. What are Chakras and Sutras, and who is Patañjali?

84. Do you bother to ask yoga teachers serious questions about their qualifications?

85. Is there any way to biblically justify the practice of yoga?

86. Is yoga connected with sorcery?

87. Have you inadvertently made an appointment with the kundalini spirit?

88. What is the real hidden purpose of yoga?

89. What are the symptoms of a kundalini syndrome?

90. Is yoga "Narcissism posing as humility"?

91. What does "I do yoga" mean?

92. Is yoga a perversity?

93. Does yoga actually deliver a "Luciferian Initiation?"

94. How can a yoga practitioner really come to Jesus?

I love reading and listening to the testimonies of those who once participated in pagan practices, but have now found their life in Jesus Christ. They are passionate about reaching those who are today in the same condition they themselves once were.

1 Corinthians 6:9-11 (NLT)
⁹ Don't you realize that those who do wrong will not inherit the Kingdom of God? Don't fool yourselves. Those who indulge in sexual sin, or who worship idols, or commit adultery, or are male prostitutes, or practice homosexuality,

[10] or are thieves, or greedy people, or drunkards, or are abusive, or cheat people—none of these will inherit the Kingdom of God.

[11] Some of you were once like that. But you were cleansed; you were made holy; you were made right with God by calling on the name of the Lord Jesus Christ and by the Spirit of our God.

The following verses sum up my prayer for you:

Psalm 119:1-3 (TPT)
[1] You're only truly happy when you walk in total integrity, walking in the light of God's word.

[2] What joy overwhelms everyone who keeps the ways of God, those who seek him as their heart's passion!

[3] They'll never do what's wrong but will always choose the paths of the Lord.

I pray you will experience the love of God in its fullness as you walk His perfect path along with His Son Jesus. I ask the Holy Spirit to fill you with wisdom, revelation, and understanding, and that you'll gain a full revelation of the Lord's unchangeable love for you. I'm confident that you'll find your place in the heavenly family, arm-in-arm with the saints and holy angels.

2

CAN YOGA EVER BE HOLY?

What? Yoga in Our Churches?

*And many false prophets will rise and will
deceive many
~ Matthew 24:11MEV*

As we approach the return of Christ, very specific prophesied markers will indicate that the great event is near. Three of the top flashing conditions that Jesus and the prophets warned us about are (1) deception[12], (2) strong delusion[13], and (3) a falling away from the true faith.[14]

In the past, I assumed these prophetic warnings were aimed primarily at evil cults, false prophets, and big-time deceivers. But Satan is subtle. He always has been (Genesis 3:1). He doesn't appear in a red outfit asking you to bow down to him. No, he convincingly introduces small suggestions on how you can get closer to God (and who doesn't want to be closer to God?). Then he introduces you to techniques that were never prescribed by God, or even forbidden by God; practices that actually lead you *away* from His presence.

What does this have to do with yoga? Let me explain.

THE YOGA QUESTION

Not too long ago, like most uninformed Americans, I thought yoga was simply a unique stretching exercise.

My wife, Mary Jo, and I enjoy our winter home located on an island in Florida. We often walk around the island and pass by a yoga studio where scores of ladies are practicing their yoga poses. Most of them seem to be fit and toned.

After walking the island one evening we strolled down to the beach to catch the breathtaking views of the Gulf of Mexico. This particular time we noticed a sign at a church offering yoga classes.

Yoga? In a church?

I can understand how something that's so trendy and popular with millions of Americans can brandish a certain appeal. What could be threatening about the practice of yoga? It's innocent enough, right?

YOGA: WHAT'S THE BIG DEAL?

Really, I thought, "What's the big deal?" I had heard the exercises were good. A Christian leader told me years ago that yoga is good if you don't do the meditations and mantras. And that was exactly my posture. That is, until I started honestly and sincerely seeking the Lord's counsel about it, and began to understand and discern some distressing concerns about so-called "Christian Yoga."

After I learned of a yoga-related "tragedy" in a minister's family, it got my attention and I wanted to find out what yoga really is and what's behind it. I began to consult Christian leaders I respected. I wanted to know if yoga played a role in the deterioration of this once beautiful family.

CHRISTIAN YOGA?

I first looked over Holy Yoga's web page and it seemed harmless, yet something in my spirit was reacting. I couldn't put my finger on it.[15]

I was troubled that the Resurrection of Jesus (the central theme of the Christian faith) was not included in Holy Yoga's stated beliefs page.

Every Christian knows the Resurrection of Jesus Christ is central to the Christian faith. It surprised me that the Resurrection of Christ was not included in the statement of beliefs on Holy Yoga's webpage.[16]

> **1 Corinthians 15:13-14**
> But if there be no resurrection of the dead, then is Christ not risen:
>
> And if Christ be not risen, then is our preaching vain, and your faith is also vain.

To its credit, the Holy Yoga website[17] provided links to the "Got Questions" website which addressed the resurrection of Christ and other basic doctrinal issues. Yet when I searched the "Got Questions" site, I found other topics addressing the subject of "Christian Yoga," and "Holy

Yoga" cautioning against its practice.[18] There were no direct links to these two pages, however, from the "Holy Yoga" web site.

Also, on the Holy Yoga web page, I found the statement that "yoga predates Hinduism." I discovered that statement to be true. Yoga predates Hinduism. Yoga actually was practiced before it became structured in pagan Hinduism, yet, based on the discovery of ancient pictographs, seems to have originated in a primitive form of pre-Vedic[19] occultism by the same eastern mystics and Shamans that introduced pre-Vedic astrology.[20]

Yoga, like astrology, was never biblically or historically a Hebrew or Christian practice. There isn't even a trace in the Bible suggesting yoga as a practice to get closer to God or "to connect with God." Neither is there a historical precedent that sanctioned the practice of yoga in either Judaism or Christianity. In fact, the opposite is true.

CHANGING THE TERMS

Marcia Montenegro of *Christian Answers for the New Age* said, "Changing the terms does not change yoga ... Just as there is no Christian Ouija board and no Christian astrology, so there is no Christian Yoga that is either truly Yoga or truly Christian."[21]

Dr. Candy Gunther Brown of Indiana University gave a forceful warning in her address to the American Society of Church History: *"Christian Yoga: Something New under the Sun/Son?"*[22] In her address, Dr. Brown discussed how many Christians are now practicing the Hindu spiritual

36

discipline of yoga and attempting to sanctify it through the use of "semantic substitution" by wrapping these practices with Christian language and Scripture.[23]

A POSE FOR DEMONS

A CBN article suggested that every yoga pose may actually be a posture of worship to one of Hindu's 330 million gods.[24] These "gods" of course are demons.

> **1 Corinthians 10:20-21 (NIV)**
> [20]...the sacrifices of pagans are offered to demons, not to God, and I do not want you to be participants with demons. 2[1] You cannot drink the cup of the Lord and the cup of demons too; you cannot have a part in both the Lord's table and the table of demons.

Dr. Laurette Willis, founder of "Praise Moves"[25] said, "These are postures that are offered to the 330 million Hindu gods. *Yoga postures really are; they are offerings to the gods.* If you do these postures and you do this breathing technique and this meditation, then you will be accepted by a god, little 'g.' That's the real danger," she said. (Laurette had been involved in yoga and the New Age for 22 years before coming to Christ).

Laurette told CBN that one of her 'Praise Moves' certified personal trainers visited India for three months on a mission trip, and "she would often see people in the streets doing yoga poses in front of the statues of the gods."[26]

"Christian Yoga...," explained Laurette. "...is like saying someone is a Christian Buddhist or a Christian Hindu. What some people are doing is that they are trying to make yoga Christian. Even Hindus are saying that you cannot do that."

SO...IS YOGA PAGAN?

As it turns out, yoga is *not* just an exercise; it is actually a pagan practice. Even Hindu Teachers say *yoga is incompatible with Christianity.*[27]

Not only CBN, but other respected ministries, like John Lindell, Mark Driscoll, Bob Larson, Chris Lawson, Jessica Smith, John Weldon, Steven Bancarz, and many solid biblical apologists, and credible Christian leaders are now warning about the dangers of Christian brands of yoga.

> **I Timothy 4:1-2 (NKJV)**
> [1] Now the Spirit expressly says that in latter times some will depart from the faith, giving heed to deceiving spirits and doctrines of demons,
> [2] speaking lies in hypocrisy, having their own conscience seared with a hot iron

WHAT IS YOGA? [28]

According to Dictionary.com, yoga is a school of Hindu philosophy prescribing a course of physical and mental disciplines for attaining union of the self with the Supreme Being or ultimate principle.

Trainees in Christian brands of yoga have evidently been coached to resist and respond to the criticism and questions about their practices. If you question them, you will predictably encounter almost identical responses and justifications, as if they are parroting a pre-planned, formulated, and perhaps a memorized rebuttal.

I have been fairly pragmatic in my 42 years of ministry and open to non-traditional and fresh tools of evangelism. Nonetheless before getting involved in or launching into anything new that I'm unfamiliar with, I want to follow four steps prior to drawing any conclusions or taking any actions:

1. Learn all I can about the issue
   (2 Timothy 2:15; Proverbs 1:5)
2. Study God's Word on the subject
   (Psalm 1:1-2; Joshua 1:8)
3. Pray to receive heaven's revelation
   (James 1:5-8; Ephesians 1:18)
4. Wait for the peace of God before I make
   a decision (Colossians 3:15; Isaiah 40:31;
   Philippians 4:7)

I followed this sequential practice while researching yoga. A couple of times in the past four decades I overlooked these four rules, and things didn't turn out so well.

YOGA AND THE OCCULT TIES

Dr. Douglas R. Groothuis is a member of the Evangelical Theological Society, Evangelical Philosophical Society, and a respected specialist on the New Age Movement. He warns Christians that yoga is not merely about physical exercise or health. *"All forms of yoga involve occult assumptions,"* he warns, *"even Hatha Yoga, which is often presented as a merely physical discipline."*[29]

God warned His people, "When you enter the land the LORD your God is giving you, be very careful *not to imitate the detestable customs* of the nations living there." (Deuteronomy 18:9 NLT)

EMBRACING PAGAN FORMS

I reviewed a paper authored by a missionary pastor in India who holds one of his graduate degrees from the Banaras Hindu University, India.

The author revealed that his wife is currently a "Holy Yoga" practitioner.[30] He argued that Paul taught we are free to embrace various pagan forms, which of course, is a gross misinterpretation of what Paul was actually writing in 1 Corinthians 9:19-23. The author wrote several wordy pages justifying the practice of yoga, speaking of its ability to bring "spiritual awareness and knowledge," and "self-realization or enlightenment" to the practitioner. Any serious student of the Bible knows that self-realization is not our goal, but our goal is to genuinely glorify God *in His prescribed manner.*

It seemed to me that the writer was suggesting that to reach Hindus and New Agers, Christians can and should adopt at least some of their practices.

Troubled, I contacted some respected leaders in India to see if they would agree. One was Silvi Siloam Kothapally, an Indian pastor and evangelist with a large ministry in India.

Here is exactly, word-for-word, what he told me: *"Yoga is totally satanic. It is the spirit of the serpent. It is very dangerous for a Christian to do yoga."*

Another Indian pastor, Sunil K. Pinninty, said, *"Yoga must be avoided. As Christians, we are not to practice yoga. In India, we do not accept yoga [in the Christian Community]."* These both are successful, stable evangelists and pastors in India.

Let's find out if it's possible that practicing yoga could bring some kind of terrifying disaster to God's people.

CHAPTER 3

WHY DISASTER COMES TO GOD'S PEOPLE

Mingling False Worship

*This disaster came upon the people of Israel because they worshiped other gods...
They had followed the practices of the pagan nations the Lord had driven from the land ahead of them... ~2 Kings 17:7, 8 (NLT)*

Israel and Judah learned that God meant what He said when He warned them not to introduce or integrate pagan practices into their worship.

The Northern Kingdom, Israel, refused to follow God's clear instructions for authentic worship and eventually adopted some of the foreign worship practices. It is quite likely that it began slowly and subtly with good intentions.

Perhaps they combined a few small practices of Baal or Asherah with the intention of appealing to the devotees of these foreign gods. This is called "syncretism."

As St. Paul later said, "A little leaven leavens the whole lump,"[31] and, over time, the people of Israel could not even recognize what true worship of God really was anymore.

Boom! Time's up! Disaster Arrives! In 722 BC, the terrorists of Assyria took over the Northern Kingdom, slaughtering many of God's people and taking many others into foreign exile and slavery.

MIXING FOREIGN PRACTICES WITH WORSHIP

This disaster came upon them *not* because of their *intentions* but because of their *practices*. This is important to note because leaders of Christian Yoga brands say things like, "Same moves—different intention." But according to God's Word, it is *not* the intention, but the practice that is the biggest danger.

> **2 Kings 17:7, 8, 9, 15 (NLT)**
> This disaster came upon the people of Israel be-
> cause they worshiped other gods...They had fol-
> lowed the *practices* of the pagan nations the Lord
> had driven from the land ahead of them, as well
> as the *practices* the kings of Israel had introduced.
> The people of Israel had also secretly done many
> things that were not pleasing to the LORD their
> God...They worshiped worthless idols, so they
> became worthless themselves. They followed the
> example of the nations around them, *disobeying the*
> *Lord's command not to imitate them.*[Emphasis mine]

The Southern Kingdom, Judah, typically enjoyed godlier kings that refused the pagan practices of other nations and thus lasted 134 years longer than the Northern Kingdom.

But as time passed, Judah too began to *incorporate foreign worship practices not prescribed by God*, and a little over a century later their time was up (just as Jeremiah prophesied in Jeremiah 25). The Babylonian hoards came in and conquered this southern kingdom, taking the people into exile and slavery for 70 years.

Why did all this happen? It's simple.

They traded true, prescribed worship and **mixed it with pagan worship**. They were not judged because of their good intentions, but because of their practice of mingling pagan traditions with true worship of the Lord. So...they lost everything.

BUT ISN'T "CHRISTIAN YOGA" DIFFERENT?

"Christian Yoga" adherents claim that it's a ministry to win people to Jesus and to relieve tensions, regulate emotions, reduce stress, etc. They tell you about people who are being helped, and even offer dramatic testimonies. But genuine Christian testimonies, at least in my opinion, are about those who came out of occult practices and are now following and testifying to the real Jesus Christ.[32]

I discovered that even Hindus recognize that "Christian Yoga" is still Hindu.[33]

One of the leaders of a "Christian" Yoga brand was advertised to speak at the Sedona Yoga Festival (a Consciousness and Evolution Festival) on the subject of "the spirituality of chakras." That's what the promotional ad announced. Chakras? We'll take a serious look at chakras and their ties to the occult later.

45

Consider this: *If Jesus allows Christians to integrate pagan traditions and occultism into Christian worship, then He is not the Jesus of Scripture.* Many of the first-century Corinthians were actually worshiping "another Jesus" and listening to a "different spirit" and **they didn't know it.** They seemed to tolerate the deception.[34]

2 Corinthians 11:4 (NKJV)
For if he who comes preaches another Jesus whom we have not preached, or if you receive a different spirit which you have not received, or a different gospel which you have not accepted—you may well put up with it!

Why are churches and pastors allowing it today? Just like me, up until recently, they probably haven't been exposed to any serious, apologetic research. Who has time to study every new trend that emerges? It's exhausting and tedious. I know, and I understand. Yet...

...Discernment is our lifeline, especially in these days of deception and delusion.

Hebrews 5:14 (NKJV)
But solid food belongs to those who are of full age, that is, those who by reason of use have their senses exercised to *discern both good and evil.*

2 Corinthians 11:3 (NKJV)
But I fear, lest somehow, as the serpent deceived Eve by his craftiness, so your minds may be corrupted from the simplicity that is in Christ.

HINDU INROADS

Back in the 1970's, Hinduism, it seems, was trying desperately to make inroads into America. They disguised their religion as "Transcendental Meditation" (TM) asserting it was *not* a religious practice. I heard all kinds of TM testimonies back then. "TM lowered my blood pressure," "helped me to have less stress," "gave me a heartfelt peace," and so on.

I remember Tom (not his real name). Tom was an anointed Bible teacher. People loved attending his classes and always walked away full of joy and filled with great biblical insights. Then Tom joined a Transcendental Meditation group to de-stress. I talked with him about it, but he snapped back with canned-sounding answers like, "It's not a religion. It's for Christians too. It's only a harmless practice to get me closer to God." Tom no longer seemed like himself.

Before long Tom ceased teaching God's Word. Instead, he was hearing voices. One of the voices told him that he had married the wrong woman and should leave her. So he responded to the voice, divorced his wife, left his family, and hooked up immediately with a "more enlightened woman."

I never saw Tom again. Many people are unaware of the fact that Transcendental Meditation is part of the yogic system, and considered to be yoga.[35]

Proverbs 14:12 (NKJV)
There is a way that seems right to a man, but its end is the way of death.

When I would warn people about Transcendental Meditation back then, it must have seemed like I was just a pharisaical nit-picker who railed against anything I didn't understand. The problem was, I *did* understand the hidden nature of Transcendental Meditation (today they call it "mindfulness") and *really was* trying to help its victims, their families, and their future. I did the same with those getting involved in other cultish groups and practices. (Acts 20:28-30)

ONE MARKER OF DECEPTION

I have an inherent, sincere desire to protect people, even if they won't listen. Yet it's almost impossible to reason with those who have given themselves over to deception. That's one of the markers of deception. But, we all have to answer to God one day, and I don't want to stand before Jesus and say, "Lord, I promoted a way to worship You that was contrary to what You prescribed in Your Word."[36] I will give account if I don't warn God's precious people about a seriously spiritual danger.

1 Peter 5:8 (ESV)
Be sober-minded; be watchful. Your adversary the devil prowls around like a roaring lion, seeking someone to devour.

It is unquestionable that yoga's roots go deep into Eastern mysticism. These roots are profoundly contrary to God and the biblical understanding of the way He works in this world. Yoga's entire philosophy is derived from pre-Vedic[37] metaphysical (mystical, esoteric, spiritual) beliefs and practices of the ancient occult shamans (sorcerers).

The word "yoga" comes from the Indian Sanskrit[38] and partially means "merger" or "union." That's why you'll hear phrases like, *"Becoming one with God"* or *"Becoming one with the universe," "Connecting with God," or "Uniting with God."*

THE SERPENT'S DECEPTION

Yoga's lies are almost identical to the serpent's lies told to Adam and Eve in Genesis 3: "For God knows that in the day you eat of it your eyes will be opened, and you will be like God, knowing good and evil (NKJV)."[39]

Incidentally, the serpent god is one of the chief deities of yoga. This spirit has been characterized as, "the counterfeit Holy Spirit" by apologists and researchers because yoga adherents actually believe they are having encounters with the Holy Spirit.

Born-again, Spirit-filled Christians hold a totally different view than the kind of worldview that lies within the practices of any type of yoga, regardless of whether or not you call it "holy" or "Christian." The entire yoga philosophy is antithetical to biblical truth.

Marcia Montenegro said it best in her 2004 article, *Yoga: From Hippies to Hip*[40]:

"Yoga has become so-well packaged as an exercise that people even believe this was the original intent of yoga, often calling yoga 'stretching exercises.'"

IS YOGA ANTI-CHRISTIAN?

"Christian Yoga is not Christian at all,"[41] says Chris Lawson of the Spiritual Research Network.

According to GotQuestions.com, "Yoga originated with a blatantly anti-Christian philosophy, and that philosophy has not changed."[42]

INDIAN CHRISTIANS WARN AGAINST YOGA

Newsweek Magazine carried an article recently where Indian Christians were warning against Christians practicing yoga.[43]

In his article, *The Subtle Body—Should Christians Practice Yoga?* Albert Mohler, Southern Baptist Seminary President, shows how there are documented ties between yoga, Transcendentalism, and New Thought (a cultish "church" movement that developed in the United States in the 19th century).

Mohler speaks honestly and directly about the incompatibility between Christianity and yoga.[44]

Once again, Apologist Chris Lawson has a great well-researched article, on Christian Yoga, entitled, *Christian Yoga: Rooted in Hindu Occultism.* [45]

"OPENING THE DOOR...TO WHAT?"

Sarah of the *Door Mouse House* blog writes, "While there may not be a 'demon behind every bush,' there genuinely are spirits, good and bad, behind every spiritual door we choose to open."

1 John 4:1 (NKJV)
Beloved, do not believe every spirit, but test the spirits, whether they are of God; because many false prophets have gone out into the world.

She continues by asking the question, "...What spirits are we potentially inviting into our lives by opening the spiritual door to our very beings through yoga?" [46]

ALTERNATIVES TO YOGA

An alternative to Christian Yoga brands may be Praise Moves.[47] There are articles on this site that will enlighten you to the dangers of yoga and also show you similar exercises that are not yoga postures. Do not confuse Praise *Moves* with Praise *Works* which allegedly is just another Christian Yoga group.

Another alternative is Pilates. It is similar to yoga, but it holds no spiritual connections to foreign deities. Be careful, however, because some yoga studios now advertise Pilates, but it is often a mixture, more like "Yogalates." Still another good alternative may be "WholyFit."[48]

So, my journey in the past few years led me from being okay with yoga, to being surprised, shocked, and embarrassed at what I didn't know about the practice.

I pray that God will fill you now with wisdom and revelation and bring you into a deep, fruitful relationship with Jesus Christ. I pray you will only consider the honor of the Lord Jesus in all you say and do in this life.

Now, let's take a closer look at the deception of Christian Yoga brands.

4

CHAPTER

CHRISTIAN YOGA:
A CLOSER LOOK

Exposing the Darkness and Deception
"Is light best friends with dark? Does Christ
go strolling with the Devil?"
~2 Corinthians 6:14, 15 MSG

What could possibly be wrong with meditating on God's Word, worshiping Jesus, listening to Christian music, and doing yoga poses at the same time?

THE JOURNEY

My journey into researching "Christian Yoga" was not to find fault, nitpick, or even warn against it. In fact, it was quite the opposite in the beginning.

I was excited to hear that participants were having "encounters with the Holy Spirit" during their holy yoga sessions. I recently heard a respected prophet say that the next big revival will bring the "rainbow" people to Jesus

53

Christ. He explained that New Age people and LGBTQ people will be repenting and turning to Christ in this next "great revival."

I believed him and had already started seeing some evidence of the beginning stages of this prophesied revival.

CAN GOD USE CHRISTIAN YOGA TO REACH HINDU YOGA ENTHUSIASTS?

A bubbling optimism existed in my heart that maybe—just maybe—Christian Yoga or holy yoga would be an instrument of God to reach the millions of New Age Hindu-style Yoga adherents in America, leading them to repentance and genuine faith in Jesus Christ.

My motivation was pure with the sincere hope that Christian Yoga, or "holy yoga" would really be anointed instruments of true evangelism. However, what I unexpectedly discovered was alarming, disturbing, and almost frightening.

I literally spent months pouring through hundreds of documents, books, and articles. I interviewed former yoga adherents and teachers.

EXPOSING DARKNESS AND DECEPTION

Exposing darkness is a tricky and often emotionally exhausting process. As followers of Jesus Christ, we must expose practices that lead to spiritual darkness, yet we don't want to hurt the sincere people who have strayed into that darkness. Our passion is to bring the light of God's Word and His Presence into dark places without wounding those who are already being harassed and injured by the prince of darkness.[49]

I would never attack the sincerity of the people involved in any kind of yoga. I would however, do my best to point out the intrinsic spiritual risks, and endeavor to speak the truth in love to these precious souls. If I myself, or someone I loved, was wandering into a hidden danger, I would be genuinely grateful for spiritually wise elders who loved me enough to tell me the truth about it.

As I reviewed hundreds of research documents, a holy fear of God descended upon me, and I found myself embarrassed by my own ignorance on the subject of yoga. I had falsely believed it was just a trendy exercise program, mostly for women.

Daily, I began asking the Lord to show me the truth and grant me His discernment. And He did just that.

To confront an issue like this is not a delight for me. You lose friends. You appear to be a critic. You get accused of being a "Pharisee." But honestly, my heart beats to honor Jesus Christ by walking in the truth and bringing His amazing love, grace, and deliverance to others.

APOLOGETICS: FAIR OR ACCUSATORY?

The work of an apologist is not something I enjoy or cherish. Apologetics is the branch of theology that defends the biblical positions of Christianity.[50] It's not about trying to win an argument, but bringing serious biblical guidance to those following unsound teachings and treacherous practices.

Honestly, I don't even like reading most materials by those who call themselves "apologists." At the same time, I realize that if the Apostle Paul had not been an apologist himself, we wouldn't have much of the New Testament we enjoy today. He confronted both doctrinal issues as well as aberrant practices that had inched their way into the Church of Jesus Christ.[51]

One reason why I dread contemporary apologetics is because some go way too far in their so-called "discernment ministries" and end up actually railing against everything they don't understand or criticizing any teaching that may differ from their particular denominational training. I never aspired to be like that.

FALSE DISCERNMENT

For example, in the 1970s when I was a young Christian, I heard from preachers and read critical papers from amateur theologians labeling Kenneth Hagin and Kenneth Copeland as false teachers. Unless I personally discovered something in their teaching that violated the fundamental truths of the Bible, or something that could jeopardize one's salvation, I made it my practice to never utter a bad word about a fellow minister or his or her ministry based on something I had heard secondhand.

When I heard the complaints and warnings about Brother Hagin's teaching I decided to listen to him to learn what he was actually saying. I did the same with Kenneth Copeland. I listened to their teachings and never once found them to be saying what the so-called "discerners" and neophyte "apologists" were telling me. Their fundamental doctrines were exactly the same as mine[52]. Yes, they talked more about faith than you would usually hear in churches, but I thought that was a good thing.

SELF-STYLED DISCERNERS

Then when the prophetic movement came along, the self-styled "discerners" and denominational apologists started sounding off again, of course against it. Without saying a word, I read Rick Joyner's books, and rather than searching for faults, I found his prophetic writings incredibly valuable and Christ-honoring. Furthermore, I found many humble, teachable souls involved in that movement. Again, they were different than we were accustomed to, but I found no egregious error or glaring doctrinal issues. They were simply trying to follow the Scriptures on prophecy, prophets, and seers. And today, we enjoy listening to these encouraging prophets like Rick Joyner, Shawn Bolz, Doug Addison, Che Ahn, Jennifer Eivaz, James Goll, Cindy Jacobs, Jennifer LeClaire, John Eckhardt, Lou Engle and others.

During the Charismatic Renewal in the 1970s, I heard an unqualified self-appointed apologist declare, *"The Charismatic Movement is a movement of the antichrist."* Yes, I actually heard that with my own ears.

That's exactly what I mean about apologists and self-styled discerners going too far.

Some apologists and discerners categorize everything into one basket. For example, they see someone speaking unintelligibly under a spell in a Hindu meeting, so they throw "speaking in tongues" into the same file and declare it to be an evil spirit. This is why you'll hear me repeatedly say, "Discernment is our lifeline in the supernatural ministry." By ignoring spiritual discernment, many promising young people who became ensnared in a deception have lost their anointing and forfeited their usefulness in God's kingdom.

When Maranatha Campus Ministries was making extensive inroads onto the campuses of America, I was told that I should preach against them. Tens of thousands were coming to Jesus through this ministry, and the students involved were vibrant and alive in the Spirit. It's true, they were more demonstrative in their form of worship than what most churches were accustomed to, but they were doctrinally sound, and their practices were not anti-biblical. After seeing God's work through Maranatha Ministries, although not part of my denomination, I decided to help them purchase their first building.

Whenever you enter something that's new, fresh, and perhaps a little different, there will be misunderstandings based on people's assumptions. Reports you hear or read may or may not be accurate.

It happened to the early twentieth century Pentecostals and every ensuing group that opened up another aspect of revelation from God's Word. With anything new or different than what I'm accustomed to I always want to be biblical and honoring to God in my research of any group being criticized.

SPIRITUALLY DANGEROUS PRACTICES

That being said, however, there are some anti-biblical, dangerous doctrines and practices that must be addressed and a warning trumpet sounded, just as St. Paul cautioned the first-century Church.

Acts 20:20-21; 28-31(NLT)
[20] I never shrank back from telling you what you needed to hear, either publicly or in your homes.

58

²¹ I have had one message for Jews and Greeks alike—the necessity of repenting from sin and turning to God, and of having faith in our Lord Jesus.

²⁸ "So guard yourselves and God's people. Feed and shepherd God's flock—his church, purchased with his own blood—over which the Holy Spirit has appointed you as elders.

²⁹ I know that false teachers, like vicious wolves, will come in among you after I leave, not sparing the flock.

³⁰ Even some men from your own group will rise up and distort the truth in order to draw a following.

³¹ Watch out! Remember the three years I was with you—my constant watch and care over you night and day, and my many tears for you.

The Apostle Paul later instructed Christians to be on the alert for the subtle introduction of another Jesus, another Spirit and another Gospel that would be tolerated and eventually welcomed into the Church. Are we seeing this happening today?

2 Corinthians 11:3-4 (NKJV)

³ But I fear, lest somehow, as the serpent deceived Eve by his craftiness, so your minds may be corrupted from the simplicity that is in Christ.

⁴ For if he who comes preaches another Jesus whom we have not preached, or if you receive a different spirit which you have not received, or a different gospel which you have not accepted—you may well put up with it!

Satan knows how to incorporate just enough truth with error to generate a deceptive falsehood, making it fiercely appealing. He's quite clever. This malevolent enemy knows very well that Spirit-filled Christians would never accept a frontal assault with occult teachings, concepts, or practices. Thus, he disguises blatant demonic doctrines by changing words to ones Christians would approve; words like, "Christian," "holy," "faith," "Yahweh," or other names that serve to mask the real spirit behind the doctrine or practice.

Because the devil typically quotes Scriptures in his deceptions (after all, that's how he approached Jesus when tempting him)[53], millions have stumbled into his traps and eventually ended up paying a price higher than they ever imagined. I know.

I served as a pastor for over thirty years and witnessed it repeatedly in the lives of those who wandered outside the boundaries of God's Word, refusing counsel and ignoring discernment. Gratefully, with God's help, I have been able to restore some of these precious souls. Unfortunately, some I have not.

James 5:19-20 (NLT)
[19] My dear brothers and sisters, if someone among you wanders away from the truth and is brought back,

[20] you can be sure that whoever brings the sinner back from wandering will save that person from death and bring about the forgiveness of many sins.

DISTINGUISHING BETWEEN HOLY AND UNHOLY

The Lord severely rebuked the leaders in Ezekiel's day for not teaching the difference between that which is holy and that which is unholy; not discerning good from evil.

Ezekiel 22:26 (NKJV)
26 Her priests have violated My law and profaned My holy things; they have not distinguished between the holy and unholy, nor have they made known the difference between the unclean and the clean...

THE POWER OF DISCERNMENT

Every believer possesses the right to exercise the power of discernment even if they don't operate in the gift of discerning of spirits. The writer of Hebrews tells us how:

Hebrews 5:14 (ESV)
But solid food is for the mature, for those who have their powers of discernment trained by constant practice to distinguish good from evil.

If we constantly practice distinguishing good from evil; holy from unholy, we will train our powers of discernment and avoid many pitfalls. I have often repeated, "Discernment is our lifeline in these days of deception, delusion, and apostasy."

NO CONDEMNATION

I don't in any manner want to shame those who have practiced or still practice some form of Christian Yoga. (There are many different names for Christian Yoga: "Holy Yoga," "Yahweh Yoga," "Praise Works Yoga," etc.) I will never accuse them of not being real Christians. That type of apologetics is not my style, and it never has been.

In fact, to be honorable in my research, I read Brooke Boon's book, *Holy Yoga*,[54] cover to cover. Boon is the creator of "Holy Yoga" with a growing network of trainers and adherents. I was very impressed with many things about Boon: her determination, business savvy, motivation, vision, and simple writing style.

While I cannot endorse her syncretistic theology, I believe she is sincere and hopes to make a difference in people's lives.

I watched several of Boon's videos in my quest to understand how a Hindu practice could possibly be integrated into the Christian faith.

IS "PRE-HINDU" YOGA SAFE FOR CHRISTIANS?

In chapter four of Boon's book, *Holy Yoga*, she addresses some of the major concerns and criticisms of yoga, yet, in my opinion, provides only fragile, shadowy explanations, at least from a biblical perspective.

For example, Boon writes, "...that yoga predates Hinduism by at least one thousand years. Yoga was not created by Hindus but was indeed co-opted by Hindus as a major part of their religion."

My question is: *What makes pre-Hindu Yoga spiritually safe?* Even in pre-Vedic times, occult practices such as astrology and numerology abounded right along with yoga. Wicca and Shamanism (both related to sorcery) date back to pre-Christian times—even as far back as 2200 B.C. to ancient

Babel (Genesis 11:1-9). However, that doesn't make it safe for Christians to practice.

Believe it or not, you can even find books and articles on the "hidden years" of Jesus which claim that Jesus traveled to India to study under the yoga masters and later secretly taught yoga to His disciples.[55]

The Huffington Post, for instance, ran an article by Paul Davids entitled, *Jesus' Lost Years May Have Been Found.*[56] The article gives highlights from *The Missing Years of Jesus* movie, also known as the *Jesus in India* movie.[57]

If Jesus went to India to learn a practice that His Father forbade, would he be the real Jesus? Or would he be a counterfeit Jesus? I think you know the answer to those questions.

The big question now is this: Can yoga be Christianized?

5

CHAPTER

CAN WE CHRISTIANIZE YOGA?

Can You Integrate an Idolatrous Practice into Christian Theology?

...because they have forsaken Me and have profaned this place by making offerings in it to other gods...
~Jeremiah 19:4 MEV

Is it possible to amalgamate a false religious practice with true Christianity?

Believing that we can Christianize yoga is like saying that we can "baptize" or "sanctify" certain occult practices and make them a part of our faith. **This is what's known as syncretism: the attempt to blend two totally incompatible philosophies or worldviews.**

Regardless of whether or not yoga predated Hinduism, yoga is still one of the six orthodox systems of the Hindu

65

religion, and has no scriptural history whatsoever in either Judaism or Christianity.

Boon, in her book, *Holy Yoga*, suggests that yoga is a "spiritual discipline like fasting, prayer, and meditation."

But "spiritual" does not necessarily mean *biblical*. Hindus are spiritual, but *not biblical*. Psychics are spiritual, yet their practices are anti-biblical. Remember, demons, too, are spiritual.

Fasting, prayer and meditation are all biblical practices; yoga *is not*. And nowhere in God's Word do we read that "yoga is a gift from God," as many Christian Yoga instructors assert.

IS YOGA AN IDOLATROUS PRACTICE?

Ezekiel 44:12-13 (MSG)
Because they acted as priests to the no-god idols and made my people Israel stumble and fall, I've taken an oath to punish them. Decree of GOD, the Master. Yes, they'll pay for what they've done. They're fired from the priesthood. No longer will they come into my presence and take care of my holy things. No more access to The Holy Place! They'll have to live with what they've done, carry the shame of their vile and obscene lives. From now on, their job is to sweep up and run errands. That's it.

What were the abominations these leaders practiced? They led God's people into idolatrous sin. These priests likely followed the current, trendy practices in Israel without consulting God's Word.

Yoga, at its core, is the idolatrous practice of a religion with over 330 million "gods," regardless of how it's repackaged. It causes sincere-hearted people to stumble and fall (v.12). The ultimate price may end up being more than anyone thought they'd have to pay (v. 12-13).

God's promises in Ezekiel 44:12 and 13 contain God's sentence for teachers who lead others into any brand of idolatry:

1. Punishment

2. High payment

3. Dismissal from ministry

4. Loss of God's presence

5. No more oversight of the *real* holy things

6. Carry shame of their actions

7. Suffer menial and petty jobs and assignments in the future

Can you integrate an idolatrous practice into Christian theology? Is it possible to take pagan practices and amalgamate them with true Christianity? Will we one day hear about:

"Christian astrology?"

"Holy psychics?"

"Godly tarot cards?"

"Holy witchcraft?"

SOLEMN CONSEQUENCES FOR MERGING DOCTRINES OR PRACTICES

God assures us that any teacher who adds to His Word or mixes in pagan practices will face solemn consequences. [58]

CORRECTION IS NEVER EASY

It's never easy to listen to correction. Our old nature tries to arise, recoil, and fire back, yet our response to sincere correction reveals our level of character.

Proverbs 15:31 (AMP)
[31] The ear that listens to and learns from the life-giving rebuke (reprimand, censure) will remain among the wise.

Whenever a Christian is confronted with the truth and listens, learns, and acts, he or she gets the honor of remaining among the wise. On the other hand, those who don't even bother to listen to reproof are biblically labeled "stupid," even though they may still consider themselves as wise.

Proverbs 12:1b (ESV)
...but he who hates reproof is stupid.

Proverbs 13:18 (ESV)
Poverty and disgrace come to him who ignores instruction, but whoever heeds reproof is honored.

WISE CHRISTIANS VALUE CORRECTION; CARELESS SCOFFERS DO NOT

Proverbs 9:8 (AMP)
Do not correct a scoffer [who foolishly ridicules and takes no responsibility for his error] or he will hate you; Correct a wise man [who learns from his error], and he will love you.

When a person hears a corrective truth, he or she will generally fall into one of four categories:

1. **Repentance.** For example, a lady who read one of the first drafts of my article on "Christian Yoga" fell on her face and repented and canceled her yoga class. She is grateful the truth came to her and wrote to thank me. I did not personally know she was practicing yoga prior to her expression of gratitude.

2. **Justification and continuation without any serious discernment.** They will still practice yoga but to appease the critics may name it something else, which in effect, actually compounds the deception. Yoga is yoga and fosters a certain spirit as we shall see in subsequent chapters. I used to jokingly refer to my fishing boat as my "yacht." But naming it something else didn't change what it really was. I can call my cat a dog, but that doesn't change what she is. You can call yoga "Christian" or "holy," but it is still yoga.

3. **Anger, accusation, and resentment.** This is when they label as "Pharisees" those who are sincerely trying to rescue them from a potentially hazardous doctrine or practice. They may even think of ways to retaliate.

4. **Grow deeper roots into the soil of the deception**. They refuse correction and dive even more deeply into the deception, coddling even

closer to a deceiving spirit. They passionately intensify their deceptive doctrine or practice to the point where they can no longer believe the actual truth of God's Word.

Rick Joyner, in his book, *The Final Quest*, speaks about his vision of three Christian armies.[59] The largest was a massive army of Christians, but everywhere they walked, the grass and vegetation turned brown and withered. They refused correction and were unteachable. Essentially, they were doing whatever they wanted without any Holy Spirit direction at all, while thinking they were doing God's work. Huge demonic vultures would defecate on these soldiers ... and they actually believed it was the anointing of the Holy Spirit. The second army had less members. Sometimes the grass turned green; sometimes brown. The next army had fewer soldiers but everywhere they went, the vegetation became green and productive. They walked with God in the fear of the Lord. This, of course is an over-simplification of Rick's vision to illustrate the point that some believers do not walk in true revelation from God, and others do.

Deception will *always* impair a person's discernment.

Acts 28:27 (NLT)
27 For the hearts of these people are hardened, and their ears cannot hear, and they have closed their eyes—so their eyes cannot see, and their ears cannot hear, and their hearts cannot understand and they <u>cannot</u> turn to me and let me heal them. (emphasis mine)

If you sincerely wish to know God's will about yoga, why not humbly kneel before Him right now and ask these questions:

1. "Lord Jesus, is yoga really Your plan for my life?"

2. "Do you want to show me something about these practices that I need to know to prevent danger in my life, my family, or my future?"

3. "Lord, will you show me a vision of my future if I continue in this practice?"

4. Then say in your own words: "Lord, I open myself to Your Spirit and Your Word for guidance in my life. If I'm on the wrong track, please show me and help me turn away from any practice that may dishonor You or jeopardize my future."

He will show you just as He has promised. (Jeremiah 33:3)

Next, let's learn about the masquerading viper who still promotes as good what God has forbidden.

IS YOGA THE SERPENT RELIGION?

The Masquerading Viper

"The serpent deceived me, and I ate."
~ Genesis 3:13

Approximately 37 million Americans practice yoga today –up significantly from 20 million just a few years ago. 75 percent of all Americans agree "yoga is good for you."[60]

So…is yoga really good for you? Or is it a demonic deception?

PROMOTING AS GOOD WHAT GOD HAS FORBIDDEN [61]

The Hebrew word in Genesis 3:1 for serpent is "*nahash*."[62] This word is used symbolically of a deadly, subtle, malicious enemy.[63]

"Nahash" is used to identify the serpent that tempted Adam and deceived Eve in the Garden of Eden where the serpent is portrayed as a deceptive creature—a con artist—who **promotes as good** what God had forbidden.

This serpent is amazingly clever in its ability to deceive the target victim. In the Book of Revelation, the serpent (also described as a dragon) is clearly identified as the devil.[64]

ORIGINS OF THE SERPENT CULT

Indian Christian leaders identify yoga as "The religion of the serpent." According to the Ancient Origins webpage,[65] "the Word" was a serpent in ancient mysticism. "Light" is what metaphorically represented a serpent known as "Kundalini."

These mystics taught that you could awaken your own divinity by performing certain practices and rituals of "the serpent people."[66]

In yoga, the student learns about the energy points on your body called "chakras." Additionally, they learn about the "kundalini" serpent of yoga, which we will discuss in a later chapter. "Chakras" and "kundalini" —these two topics alone, when understood, provide a dead giveaway as to the real spiritual nature of yoga.

THE MASQUERADING VIPER

Satan, the serpent, is a great masquerader and imposter. "The Word" is a biblical term used for Jesus Christ (God's Son)[67], *not* the serpent, as the ancient mystics taught. Jesus is also identified as "The Light of men" and a "Light that shines in the darkness," *not* the "kundalini."[68]

In early schools of occult mysticism, the serpent is described as "The Word" and the "light." This is an exposure of a truth hidden in plain sight. And it's this: **the devil is a counterfeiter.**

> **2 Corinthians 11:13-15 (KJV)**
> [13] For such are false apostles, deceitful workers, transforming themselves into the apostles of Christ.
>
> [14] And no marvel; for Satan himself is transformed into an angel of light.
>
> [15] Therefore it is no great thing if his ministers also be transformed as the ministers of righteousness; whose end shall be according to their works.

THE COMING ANTICHRIST

One day, perhaps soon, there will arrive on the world scene a counterfeit Christ. The Bible calls him "the Antichrist," "the beast," and "the lawless one."[69]

Satan's highest ambition is to be like God in power, authority, and control. He works hard in three areas: (1) temptation, (2) deception, and (3) accusation to achieve his goals. During the tribulation period spoken of by Jesus, a man will arise, "Who opposes and exalts himself above all that is called God, or that is worshipped, so that he sits as God in the temple of God, showing himself that he is God."[70]

His intention is to replace God. The antichrist will worship the "god of forces," or "energies," or "fortresses."[71]

Not surprisingly, Hindus also are looking for such a world leader to arise.[72]

YOGA DEITY, VISHNU, TO BRING "AGE OF TRUTH"

Hindus believe that a leader called "the Kalki" will rise to power with the promise of bringing peace. Kalki, they believe, will be the final incarnation of Vishnu *(one of the three gods of yoga)* who will establish the "Age of Truth and Purity" on Earth.

Over 6,000 verses in the Indian Sanskrit detail the life of "Kalki." He is known as "The Awaited One who will *not* be a man of peace like Jesus Christ or Buddha but a man of war who will destroy evil and establish righteousness on the earth." They speak of "Signs of the Koli Age" and the coming appearance of Kalki.[73]

THE RELIGION OF ANTICHRIST

"The practice of yoga is pagan at best, and occult at worst. This is the religion of antichrist and for the first time in history it is being wildly practiced throughout the Western world and America. It is ridiculous that even yogi masters wearing a Cross or a Christian symbol deceive people saying that yoga has nothing to do with Hinduism and say that it is only accepting the other cultures. Some have masked yoga with Christian gestures and call it "Christian Yoga." [74]   ~*James Manjackal MSFS*

Father Manjackal also reported that yoga can actually lead to demon possession. He shared his personal yoga testimony in an article entitled "Yoga Leads to Idolatry and Possession."[75]

Satan knows God's prophetic plan for the future. That's likely the reason behind his frantic promoting of an array of perverse ideas and forbidden practices today. He's making a last-ditch effort to confuse and deceive humankind, to prevent them from experiencing the true Jesus Christ by enticing them to run after counterfeits.[76]

If you study the beliefs of Eastern religions you quickly realize that people can actually "become one" with a demonic entity. Pagan kings who claimed "divinity" became yoked with a demonic deity. For example, King Nebuchadnezzar had ordered people to bow to his own image, threatening a fiery death to those who refused to bow. One year later, the king went insane, walking like an animal and eating grass like a cow.[77]

A New Testament instance of this is that of King Herod the Great who accepted the glory that was due only to God.

Acts 12:23 (NLT)
Instantly, an angel of the Lord struck Herod with a sickness, because he accepted the people's worship instead of giving the glory to God. So he was consumed with worms and died.

Doctors have recently identified what killed this man at age 69, as reported by ABC News. He was stricken with a chronic kidney disease complicated by an excruciatingly painful case of maggot-infested gangrene of the genitals.[78]

There seems to be an extravagant price for connecting with the wrong spirits.

The prophesied Antichrist himself will "become one" with his deity (the god of forces, powers, energies) known as "The Beast, Abaddon, and Apollyon." [79] And his days will be numbered, just as King Herod's were (Revelation 19:20).

MENTAL ILLNESS IN AMERICAN CULTURE

I listened to a fascinating interview with Arthur Burk of the Sapphire Leadership Group.[80] The host of the program asked Arthur why there was so much mental illness in American culture today.[81] Arthur gave the three biggest reasons:

1. **"Hippie culture from the 1960s: Rebellion"** A massive number of angry hippies never got reconciled to themselves, their families, or the culture." *(Rebellion is the same as the sin of witchcraft - 1 Samuel 15:23.)*

2. **"Massive embracing of Eastern occult practices."** *(This, of course, began with the introduction of yoga and other forms of mysticism to American people. They've done an effective job if truly 75 percent of Americans believe that yoga is good for you.)*

3. **"Big Pharma,** which has become increasingly amazing with their miraculous resources...and [increasingly] dark at the same time as some really unholy things are taking place." *(Even prescription drugs can have an effect on our thinking and feeling.)*

EXPERT SAYS YOGA LAYS THE FOUNDATION FOR OCCULTISM

Yoga scholar and Sanskrit authority, Rammurti Mishra, interprets yoga as laying the foundation for occultism.

Mishra believes that behind mysticism and occultism, the Yoga system is present, whether one realizes it or not.[82]

A Messianic Jewish Ministry, Shalach Ministries, warns that "Regardless of the school or spiritual tradition, **Yoga practice tends to alter a person's consciousness in an occult direction.**"[83]

In the book *Psychic Forces and Occult Shock*, Wilson and Weldon state, "Yoga is really pure occultism, as any number of yoga and occult texts prove."[84]

Kurt Koch, in his book, *Christian Counseling and Occultism: A Complete Guidebook to Occult Oppression and Deliverance*, wrote, "Occult abilities are very common from yoga practice, and the numerous dangers of occultism are evident from many studies."[85]

Koch in his various excellent books correlates involvement in the occult practices with subsequent experiences of anxiety and depression sometimes resulting in suicide.[86]

THE END-TIME OCCULT INVASION

Apologist Eric Barger,[87] who co-hosted Jan Markell's radio program, *Understanding the Times,* [88] which addressed "Holy Yoga" and other forms of yoga, calls the occult phenomena we are seeing in the Western World, "The end-time occult invasion." He says, "Every aspect of the world of the occult appears now to be normalized."

"It has invaded our culture to make the occult look normal."

Eric continues, "[Occultism] is being practiced in our communities in places where we never dreamed we'd see it. We seem to trivialize it; we seem not to be bothered by it."

HAS THE SERPENT ENTERED THE CHURCH?

Years ago, I went downstairs to do some laundry. I saw one of my socks moving around on top of the clothes dryer, so I pulled back the socks and some other laundry items and was shocked to find two snakes under the small pile of clothes. I jumped back and probably let out a frightening scream. Fortunately, they were harmless garter snakes, nonetheless startling.

Do you think I was going to leave these snakes in my home? No, of course not. Even non-venomous snakes emit an odor that can be harmful to humans over time. I noticed the snakes seemed to be sick and slow. Then I remembered a pest controller, just hours before, came to spray some hornets' nests around our house. I figured the snakes must have become sick because of the pesticide, so I picked them up and placed them in a safe enclosed environment outside the house until they recovered. I like garter snakes outside because they keep small rodents away, but I don't want them inside my house.

Lukas Alpert, staff writer for the Daily News wrote an exceptional article entitled, "Snake house of horrors: Idaho family driven from home after finding thousands of serpents."

A lovely young family bought a beautiful sprawling house in Idaho in 2009, but when they moved in they discovered the house was infested with thousands of garter snakes.[89] Every day the family was faced with snakes in their home, slithering inside the walls, on the floors, and in the laundry room. Daily, they would fight off the snakes, sometimes carrying out twenty or thirty at a time. But nothing stopped the infestation. With two small children and the wife being pregnant, the snakes finally won the battle, and the family moved out after only three months. No sane person wants snakes —even garter snakes—in their home.

They said, "It felt like it was Satan's lair."[90]

The *Fatal Attractions* television program presented a documentary entitled "*Snakes in a Trailer*" about a lady who passionately loved snakes.[91] She thought she understood their feelings and believed they understood and loved her too. She felt a strong connection to snakes of all kinds, even keeping rattlesnakes in her mobile home, treating them as adorable pets. Once she was bitten by a venomous snake, but experienced no adverse reaction, which caused her to believe she was immune to snake venom.

Somehow this lady bought an exotic deadly venomous asp which she kept in an aquarium-like house. She would let the snakes out of their caged "homes" while cleaning them. One day she let the deadly viper go free in the house so she could clean its little snake home. When she finished cleaning she searched for the viper and couldn't find it. But when she reached under the furniture it struck her. She died within 30 minutes, blood coming out of her nose, eyes, ears, mouth, and other places. The snake won.

Revelation 12:9 (ESV)
And the great dragon was thrown down, that ancient serpent, who is called the devil and Satan, the deceiver of the whole world—he was thrown down to the earth, and his angels were thrown down with him.

WAS THIS A PROPHETIC DREAM?

My daughter, who has in recent years has become remarkably prophetic, experienced a vivid dream warning about the serpent-dragon coming into the Church. I know dreams are profoundly subjective and can be the result of brain chemicals from certain foods. Nonetheless, spiritual dreams are quite prominent in Scripture,[92] and visions and dreams are prophesied in Joel 2 and Acts 2 as a feature of the last days.

When I was pastor of Mount Hope Church in Lansing, Michigan, we often presented beautiful musical pageants such as *The Passion Play* and other biblical presentations. The sound, music, lighting, singing, acting, and brilliant colors were all majestic and Christ-honoring. One year over 16,000 people visited to view that year's version of *The Passion Play*.

My daughter's dream concerned a pageant at our church. She was sitting in the audience enjoying the flags, the banners, the music, and the emotion of the production. But when it came to the scene that reenacted Palm Sunday, the most festive and vibrant celebration of Jesus, she saw something that stunned her to the core.

In the midst of the colorful and celebratory pageantry, some of the leaders joined in with a huge paper serpent-dragon, much as you would see in an Eastern oriental parade. The Japanese call it a "Tatsuo," which is a serpent-like dragon. These leaders brought the gigantic Tatsuo onto the platform making it move and slither with the attached sticks, like you see in Eastern world celebrations. But this was supposed to be Palm Sunday, not an Eastern world parade.

My daughter started screaming, "No! Why are they bringing that thing into the production?" She cried out to Jesus, and suddenly the paper serpent-like dragon fell down onto the platform, covering three of the specific leaders of the event.

Those who carried the paper Tatso into the sanctuary were now under it. My daughter told me that nobody was physically hurt in the dream; they were just underneath this hideous prop.

She sensed this was a spiritual dream and somehow prophetic. I felt the same.

I was happy to learn that in her dream the people who transported and operated this Tatsuo in the church were not physically hurt by it. They were okay, yet they, themselves were covered by this paper serpent-dragon.

As I've already said, *dreams are subjective*. Yet, God can still speak through dreams to encourage intercession, prompt a change in direction, or bring you confirmation. This dream my daughter shared with me seemed to be prophetic in some way.

I began to ask some sincere questions:

1. By Christians embracing Eastern occult practices like yoga, is it possible that their God-given destiny in His Kingdom could be masked or veiled, just as the paper Tatsuo covered its supporters?

2. Could these Eastern practices actually cap their ability to see the reality of the living God and to receive His gentle guidance and direction for their lives?

3. I noticed also that when my daughter cried out to Jesus, the paper serpent fell to the floor. I wondered if God was giving her a lesson in the power of intercession to bring down deceptions that are scheming their way into our churches. Intercessors arise! You have the power to enforce purity and God's honor in your church.

4. Could the paper serpent-dragon be veiling or muting their anointing and leading them from one dead-end to another in their lives and ministries? After all, biblically, this is precisely what happened to God's people, Israel, every time they syncretized their faith in God with pagan philosophies and practices.

Psalm 37:38 (MSG)
But the willful will soon be discarded; insolent souls are on a dead-end street.

And this also was the identical result of King Saul's defiance of God's instructions. He finally came to his "dead-end" street, and the picture was not pretty.

1 Samuel 15:23 (NKJV)
For rebellion is as the sin of witchcraft, and stubbornness is as iniquity and idolatry. Because you have rejected the word of the Lord, He also has

rejected you from being king.

Rebellion is as the sin of witchcraft. Those who are spiritually alive, submitted to Jesus Christ, and surrendered to the will of God will see and understand the truth. Those living in some kind of rebellion will not perceive the truth.

I have come to believe five things about professing Christians who practice yoga:

1. Yoga (in any form) can disrupt your discernment.

2. Yoga (in any form) can corrupt your destiny.

3. Yoga (in any form) can impair your anointing.

4. Yoga (in any form) can sabotage your calling.

5. Yoga (in any form) can subvert your future.

Some believe that Christian Yoga brands are different and safe...but is that true?

7
CHAPTER

BUT...ISN'T CHRISTIAN YOGA DIFFERENT?

"Every Plant Which My Heavenly Father Did Not Plant Will Be Torn Up By The Roots."

They shall teach My people the difference between the holy and profane, and cause them to discern between the unclean and the clean.
~ Ezekiel 44:23

People constantly ask, "But...isn't there a difference in Christian Yoga?"

After literally hundreds, perhaps thousands, of hours of investigating the practice of yoga and analyzing this contemporary trend of so-called "Christian Yoga," I have reached the conclusion that, at the core, there is *no spiritual distinction whatsoever* between "Christian Yoga" and "Hindu Yoga."

Yoga is yoga. Hatha Yoga is Hatha Yoga whether or not you call it "Faith Hatha" or any other kind of "faith-y" or holy name. There may be different music or different meditations or different intentions, but the spirit behind it is the same. *If the fundamental roots are evil, the tree will be evil.*

Matthew 15:13 (AMP)
He answered, "Every plant which My heavenly Father did not plant will be torn up by the roots."

Yoga was not planted by the heavenly Father, but by occult shamans and sorcerers. It was later incorporated into the Hindu religion and is now being exported and disguised as a stress-breaking, healthy exercise.

The heavenly Father did not plant yoga, grow yoga, promote yoga, give yoga as a gift, or wink at the religion of yoga[93]. Yet Western Hindu "evangelists" are popping up in communities and churches in America and Europe proclaiming that "nobody owns yoga" and we can include it with our Christian practice. Please read the parable of Jesus in Matthew 13:24-30; 36-43.

FILLING THE LAND WITH PRACTICES FROM THE EAST

Why God was forced to reject His own people

Isaiah 2:5-6 (NLT)
5 Come, descendants of Jacob, let us walk in the light of the Lord!
6 For the Lord has rejected his people, the descendants of Jacob, because they have filled their land with practices from the East and with sorcerers, as the Philistines do. They have made alliances with pagans.

Here are a few good questions:

1. Do you believe that maybe—just maybe—God views every yoga studio and every yoga session as a shrine to a pagan deity?

2. Does yoga appear to you to be an idolatrous practice with roots in ancient occultism?

3. Can yoga—any brand of yoga—attract a dangerous serpent spirit, known as "kundalini," the spirit that perceptive discerners recognize as "the counterfeit Holy Spirit?"

YOGA DISRUPTS CHRISTIAN FAITH

The managing editor of *Hinduism Today*, Sannyasin Arumugaswami, remarked that Christians trying to adapt to yogic practices will likely disrupt their own Christian beliefs.[94]

An instructor named Danda likewise stated in an e-mail to Lighthouse Trails Research that Yoga is a religion that denies Jesus Christ and has nothing to do with Jesus.[95]

He continued by kindly saying, "We appreciate when others understand that all of **Yoga is all about the Hindu religion.**"[96]

YOGA IS "JUST AN EXERCISE," RIGHT?

Do you know the identity of the real lord of yoga? The real lord of yoga is a Hindu demon-god named "Shiva." This demon-god is just one of the gods to which yoga postures were formed to venerate.

Who is Shiva? The "lord of yoga" is known as "Shiva, the destroyer" and "the god of death."

God gave us His Holy Word and His Holy Spirit. He never gave us holy yoga or holy sorcery.

Do you want a house full of spiritual snakes? Would you want even garter snakes in your home or in your church? Snakes are popularly associated with both Vishnu and Shiva, two of the three "gods" of yoga.

Michael Lofton, in the article, "Awakening the Serpent Within—Yoga, an Invitation to Demonic Possession,"[97] writes:

"To the Christian, the greatest danger is the spiritual idolatry, before God, in engaging in practices devised thousands of years ago by pagan experts or 'adepts,' to become "united" with spiritual deity, they believed to be the 'Absolute,' or 'Ultimate Reality,' but which the Bible calls 'fallen angels' or demons."[98]

If you have practiced yoga or some kind of so-called "Christian Yoga," it doesn't mean you are an evil person. It simply means you believed someone who told you that "because it's only Hatha Yoga, it's spiritually safe."

The serpent's tactics have not changed in all these thousands of years since Adam and Eve. *He promotes as good what God has forbidden.*

You may want to repent before the Lord right now, asking His forgiveness and restoration if you have practiced any form of yoga. Tell Him in your own words how sorry you are for engaging in a forbidden practice that honors false gods. In Jesus' Name, command any demonic attachment you may have accidentally picked up through the yogic practice to go. Now, really stay connected with God *only* through Jesus Christ.

Yoga is not merely an exercise. It is a spiritual system that transmits a certain spirit.

8

THE SPIRITUAL
SYSTEM OF YOGA

Carrying and Transmitting a Certain Spirit and Culture

Beloved, do not believe every spirit, but test the spirits to see whether they are from God ...
~ 1 John 4:1 MEV

Most of us in America, as well as the entire Western world, have heard of yoga.

A majority of Americans and Europeans view it as a mere physical exercise or just a harmless practice that fitness buffs enjoy doing.

But it's more than that. Yoga is a spiritual discipline. Even "Holy Yoga" admits to being a spiritual discipline "much like fasting, meditation, and prayer."[99]

In a later chapter we'll look at the sexual system of yoga,

but for now, let's learn more about this **spiritual system** called "yoga."

We have learned that yoga, as we know it today, originated in ancient India, although its earliest roots likely go all the way back to Babylon (Babel). Yoga was practiced in primitive occult shamanism. In fact, the pagan nations that God drove out of the land of Israel practiced polytheism (many gods) or pantheism (God is in everything), which later grew into modern Hinduism. The Hindus formulated the practice by incorporating the Yoga Sutras into their religion, making yoga one of their six fundamental doctrines. Today yoga is a religious and spiritual practice in Hinduism.

Yoga's literal meaning is to 'yoke,' 'join,' 'unite,' or 'attach.' When a person does yoga poses, he or she is *uniting* or being *yoked* with some entity.

The word "yoga" does not mean unity, as in "unity of the faith" or "unity of the Holy Spirit" but connotes a yoking as in *attaching to a spiritual being, energy or essence; joining with the characteristics of that invisible being or thing*.

It's true when a Christian Yoga instructor tells you that yoga is a "spiritual discipline." In fact, yoga is *more spiritual than physical*.

Hindus hold many objects and ideas as sacred or holy. They believe and teach that icons and statues contain the essence, or energy of the deities they represent. That's why you'll see them anointing their holy icons and statues and performing yoga poses before them. In this way, they believe they can connect with the unique characteristics and energies of the sacred "god" to which they are bowing.[100]

You may be familiar with the fact that Hindus venerate holy animals, holy icons, holy rivers, holy saints, and holy cities as well.[101]

To the Christian and Jew, holy means something totally different. The Hebrew word for holy is "qodesh" which means "set-apartness" and to be "otherness" or different than others.

God's people were to think, act, and worship differently than other cultures, other religions, and other conflicting worldviews. The Hebrew word "qodesh" is used over 400 times in the Old Testament to describe the nature of God and as an objective for His own people.

The New Testament Greek word for holy is "hagios." It is used 180 times in the New Testament and means to be "set apart."

God Himself is set apart from all other so-called gods. He is the only true God. **Believers are warned not to attempt to mix Him with other gods, or with the practices of the other gods** (which are really demons, according to St. Paul).[102]

To the Hindu, yoga is one path to holiness and uniting with their god or "god consciousness." To the Christian, "holiness is not the way to God; Jesus is the way to God and also the way to authentic holiness." [103]

The gods of other religions are not just names or myths, but demonic beings who love accepting worship, taking what rightfully belongs only to the One True God.

Yoga *in any form* is spiritual. It, therefore, carries and transmits a certain spirit.

There is nothing honestly holy about yoga to Christians. The truth is, yoga is not holy at all and it certainly is not Christian. "Christian Yoga" brands, it seems to me, are really little more than basic Hinduism airbrushed with a thin veneer of Christian cosmetics.

YOGA: A TYPE OF SPIRITUALISM

An article I read recently was positive toward the practice of yoga. In its content, however, the writer admitted, **"Yoga is rooted in spiritualism,** and many of the postures have a meaning that goes beyond simple strengthening and lengthening of muscles." [104]

What is spiritualism? Sometimes it's called "spiritism." It is the belief or doctrine that the spirits of the dead can and do communicate with the living, especially through a medium.

Spiritualism (or spiritism) was among God's forbidden pagan practices.

King Manasseh (687–642 BC) "...practiced soothsaying, used witchcraft and sorcery, and consulted mediums and spiritists. He did much evil in the sight of the Lord, to provoke Him to anger." [105]

In Hinduism, this spiritism is a little different, but nonetheless still spiritism. The contacting or connecting in yoga is not with dead souls as in Spiritualism, but with the deities of Hinduism. Interest in Eastern Spiritualism and yoga in the Western world soared in the 1960s during the hippie movement.

DISRUPTING AND SHIPWRECKING CHRISTIAN FAITH

By accepting and practicing the false disciplines of pagan religions, you can unsettle and even decimate your faith in Christ. The Apostle Paul wrote to his son in the faith, Timothy, explaining how some people actually shipwreck their faith by rejecting real faith and a good conscience.

1 Timothy 1:18-20 (NKJV)

[18] This charge I commit to you, son Timothy, according to the prophecies previously made concerning you, that by them you may wage the good warfare,

[19] having faith and a good conscience, which some having rejected, concerning the faith have suffered shipwreck,

[20] of whom are Hymenaeus and Alexander, whom I delivered to Satan that they may learn not to blaspheme.

HATHA YOGA—A SPRINGBOARD TO DEEP DECEPTION

Hatha Yoga is the type most "Christian Yoga" teachers tout. But what the student may not know is that Hatha Yoga was designed to provide an entry point with the links necessary for descending into deeper encounters that lead to spiritual deception and possibly delusion. According to the Classical Yoga Hindu Academy, Hatha Yoga actually provides "worshipful postures and an integral link in the Hindu religion."[106]

Hatha Yoga was designed to offer Hindu devotional postures.[107] Hatha   Yoga (stretching, breathing, and relaxation exercises) actually provides the worship poses of Hinduism.[108] Hatha Yoga offers the springboard to a progressive, step-by-step process into the Eastern religious/spiritual path. In other words, Hatha Yoga is an entry point into polytheism, pantheism, spirit-ism, and the realm of the demonic.

Many hold the notion that yoga is spiritual but not religious. According to the Classical Yoga Hindu Academy, "It is a totally false statement that Yoga is not religion."[109]

According to the *Hatha Yoga Pradipika*, the basic purpose of Hatha Yoga is to "purify the Ida and Pingala Nadis and then uniting these two forces with the third Psychic Nadi Sushumna, which carries Kundalini at Ajna Chakra (eyebrow center)."[110]

New Age Yoga in America and the Western world is really Hinduism in disguise.

There are catch phrases, or talking points used by New Age Yoga teachers as well as Christian Yoga teachers. These may surprise you, but will assist you in using greater discernment in the days ahead. That's what we'll look at next.

9

CHAPTER

PHRASES IDENTIFYING
NEW AGE (OCCULT) YOGA

The Seeds of Eastern Mysticism Have Already Been Planted

...They have filled their land with practices from the East and with sorcerers...they have made alliances with pagans.
~ Isaiah 2:6b NLT

Shortly before he went to heaven, I talked with Mark Buntain, the well-known, iconic missionary to India. He and his wife Huldah are best known for founding a prominent hospital and feeding ministry in Calcutta that brought tens of thousands to Jesus Christ.

We sat for lunch at the Hoffman House Restaurant in Lansing, Michigan, when Mark looked up at me with deep concern on his face and said, "Pastor Dave, if I could only preach one message in America for the rest of my life, it would be a sermon about how the New Age Movement—like a brood of vipers—is infiltrating the nation...and the Church." That was in March of 1988, long before "Holy Yoga," "Christian Yoga." "Yahweh Yoga," "Praise Works Yoga," or any of the contemporary faith-type yoga classes had made their debuts.

But the seeds of Eastern Mysticism had already been planted in the 1950s by Paramahansa Yogananda, hailed as the "father of Yoga in the West." Yogananda founded The Self-Realization Fellowship to disseminate his writings including his book, *The Yoga of Jesus—Understanding the Hidden Teachings of the Gospels.* This was the first book, to my knowledge, that attempted to convince Christians that yoga could be added to their faith. His peculiar and bizarre interpretations of Gospel truths would stun anyone who is a faithful student of God's Word, and confuse others who had little Bible knowledge.[111]

New Agers are greatly influenced by Eastern thought and Eastern practices such as those Yogananda taught.

The following are New Age clichés about yoga. These statements or similar ones are found in New Age Yoga literature, and unfortunately on many of the Christian Yoga brands' web pages too.

1. New Agers say, **"Yoga is simply a physical exercise. Yoga is not a religion."**
   The Truth: Those who understand yoga know this New Age statement is untrue. According to the Classical Yoga Hindu Academy, "...To say 'I

do yoga' is like saying 'I do spiritual union,' or 'I do religion.'" [112]
Saying that yoga is just an exercise would be like saying Holy Communion is nothing but a wine tasting event.[113]

2. New Agers say, **"I am spiritual but not religious."**
The Truth: Yoga is both spiritual and religious and involves the worship of other gods, even though the participant may not realize it. Yoga is spiritual and overtly (and sometimes covertly) prompts the worship of other gods (demons). If that is true, the practice of yoga—any kind of yoga is therefore idolatry.

3. New Agers say, **"Yoga is a science; not a religion."**
The Truth: The doctrine behind yoga is Hindu polytheism or sometimes pantheism. Polytheism points to many gods. Pantheism identifies God with the universe or often regards the universe as "a manifestation of God." Polytheism and pantheism were the religions of the Canaanites who were driven from their land by those who worshipped the One True and Living God. According to the Classical Yoga Hindu Academy, yoga is NOT a science at all, but a religion. If yoga were a science, there would be university classes in the "Science of Yoga."

4. New Agers say, **"Following yoga will help you better understand your religion."**
The Truth: This is the same lie used in the effort to market Transcendental Meditation. Yoga actually dulls one's ability to discern the truth. It opens a practitioner to deception from Satan who searches for victims to lure away from God.

5. New Agers say, **"Religion has rules and rituals; yoga has none of these."**

6. New Agers say, **"Spirituality unites and religion divides."**
The Truth: Yoga unites. That is a fact. It yokes a practitioner to a Hindu deity.
Corinna Craft, for instance, really believed she could integrate yoga with her Christian beliefs and that she could not be deceived because Jesus would protect her. Slowly she discovered that demons began manipulating her life. She had become yoked with an entity that influenced and tried to destroy her life...until she received deliverance from the Savior. She entitles her testimony, **"Deliverance from a Demon of Yoga**[114]**,"** and sums up the practice of Christian Yoga with these words:
"Put in starker terms, *the mat is the altar, the practitioner is the sacrifice, and those who feed on the practitioner are Hindu demons."* She continued, "Yoga, at the very least, opens a

Christian to demonic influence and at worst, demonization."[115]

7. New Agers say, **"Spirituality is God-made and religion is man-made."** How many times have you heard this?

8. New Agers say, **"Nobody owns Yoga."** The Truth: This sounds mysteriously familiar to statements Christian Yoga teachers make. Holy Yoga's website states: "We know that yoga is a spiritual discipline much like fasting, meditation, and prayer that cannot be owned by one specific religion."[116]

150 STOLEN (PIRATED) YOGA POSES

Is it true that "yoga cannot be owned by one specific religion?"

David Orr of the Washington Times wrote a shocking article entitled, **"India Makes Moves to Reclaim Heritage from 'Yoga Piracy.'"**[117] According to the article, the Indian government has become so concerned with the pirating of copyrighted yoga poses, they established a task force to investigate yoga pirating. Yoga postures apparently *are* owned by Indian Hindus.

"Yoga piracy is becoming very common, and we are moving to do something about it," says Vinod Gupta, the head of a recently established Indian government task force on traditional knowledge and intellectual-property theft.

The Indian government has discovered at least 150 copyrighted asanas (yoga postures) have been pirated in the Western world, including the United States.

The article goes on to say, "In an effort to protect India's heritage, the task force has begun documenting 1,500 yoga postures drawn from classical yoga texts—including the writings of the Indian sage, Patañjali, the first man to codify the art of yoga."[118]

ARE LAWSUITS COMING TO WESTERN WORLD YOGA TEACHERS?

To boast "nobody owns yoga" may eventually prove to be false when and if Indian investigators begin their lawsuits against yoga studios for international copyright piracy.

I interviewed a former Holy Yoga participant in Florida who told me that her yoga teacher taught that push-ups were actually yoga poses. Are you serious? I guess if they can commandeer copyrighted Hindu poses claiming "no religion owns yoga," they could also hijack legitimate exercises and claim them to be yoga.

CHRISTIAN YOGA PRACTITIONERS JUSTIFY THEM-SELVES

Yoga teachers instruct students to focus on their inner selves rather than focusing on the One True God.

In listening to those who practice "Christian Yoga," you'll quite often hear justifications such as: "I love the way it makes *me* feel," or "It helps connect *me* to Jesus." The focus is on "*me*" rather than on what God really says in His Word, the Bible.

"But we meditate on the Bible and listen to Christian music while doing our yoga poses," they protest.

If that's the case, have you meditated on the following Scriptures during yoga practice? Maybe if you did the Lord would touch your heart and give you a revelation about the true nature and character of every brand of yoga.

2 Thessalonians 2:11-12 (NKJV)
[11] And for this reason God will send them strong delusion, that they should believe the lie,

[12] that they all may be condemned who did not believe the truth but had pleasure in unrighteousness.

Romans 1:21-23 (NLT)
[21] Yes, they knew God, but they wouldn't worship him as God or even give him thanks. And they began to think up foolish ideas of what God was like. As a result, their minds became dark and confused.

[22] Claiming to be wise, they instead became utter fools.

[23] And instead of worshiping the glorious, ever-living God, they worshiped idols made to look like mere people and birds and animals and reptiles.

[24] So God abandoned them to do whatever shameful things their hearts desired.

Ezekiel 22:26 (NKJV)
Her priests have violated My law and profaned My holy things; they have not distinguished between the holy and unholy, nor have they made known the difference between the unclean and the clean

2 Corinthians 11:13-15 (NKJV)
[13] For such *are* false apostles, deceitful workers, transforming themselves into apostles of Christ. [14] And no wonder! For Satan himself transforms himself into an angel of light.

[15] Therefore it is no great thing if his ministers also transform themselves into ministers of righteousness, whose end will be according to their works.

Regardless of your intention, you cannot separate the yoga poses from the Eastern philosophy.

NO SUCH THING AS NEUTRAL YOGA

Author and speaker, Johanna Michaelsen was for years involved in the occult, yoga, and Silva Mind Control. She now absolutely rejects all such practices. Johanna Michaelsen is a noted author, researcher, lecturer and authority on the occult. Appearing on several Christian and secular television programs, TBN, CBN, Jack Van Impe, John Ankerberg and dozens more, she began to stir the ire of those who refused to believe the power of the occult and yoga, and found herself a target of critics, yet continued to boldly speak out for God.

Michaelson wrote concerning yoga, "You cannot separate the exercises from the philosophy...The movements themselves become a form of meditation. The continued practice of the exercises will, whether you...intend it or not, eventually influence you toward an Eastern/mystical perspective. That is what it is meant to do!...There is, by definition, no such thing as 'neutral' Yoga" (*Like Lambs to the Slaughter*, pp. 93-95).[119]

In the same manner Pastor John Lindell was attacked after preaching the truth about yoga, Michaelson has also faced her own barrage of critics. When people don't like the message, they always seem to find a way to attack the messenger.

History repeats itself. The Bible is full of examples from the beginning of time where God's prophets and messengers were attacked by those who chose to reject a warning or instruction from God. In time, these rejecters suffered the dreadful consequences.

Jeremiah 7:24 (NLT)
²⁴ "But my people would not listen to me. They kept doing whatever they wanted, following the stubborn desires of their evil hearts. They went backward instead of forward.

Jesus prophesied concerning the last days, "But of that day and hour no one knows, not even the angels of heaven, but My Father only. But as the days of Noah were, so also will the coming of the Son of Man be. For as in the days before the flood, they were eating and drinking, marrying and giving in marriage, until the day that Noah entered the ark (Matthew 24:36-38 NKJV).

One thing for certain: people rejected Noah's preaching. Suddenly, it became too late.

Here's the reality: the dark spirit realm has ownership rights over yoga.

Next, we will talk about the "intention" in practicing yoga.

10
CHAPTER

IS IT REALLY THE 'INTENTION' THAT MATTERS?

Can Christians Participate In a Hindu Religious Exercise With The Right Intention and Make It Holy?

...you also, as living stones, are being built up into a spiritual house as a holy priesthood to offer up spiritual sacrifices that are acceptable to God through Jesus Christ. ~ 1 Peter 2:5 MEV

Here is a statement I read on the "Holy Yoga" webpage: "God looks at the heart and not the body. It always comes down to intentionality." The Frisco Holy Yoga site uses a similar phrase by advertising, *"Same Postures, Different Intention."*[120]

In Chapter two of Brooke Boon's book, *Holy Yoga*, she

states, "While yoga cannot be considered a "classical" Christian discipline, it nevertheless has the same goal and can have similar effects as other disciplines, provided it is practiced with the right intent."[121]

The question is this: Can a Christian participate in a Hindu religious exercise with the right intention and make it holy?

When God's judgment arrived on His people, it never came because of intention. Judgment fell because of their practices, particularly when they began mixing the practices of pagan religions with their worship of the Only True God. Prophets warned about the detestable practices of pagan religions, but the people seemed to believe that if their intention was pure, it was acceptable.

King Manasseh, for example, employed the same practices as the pagan nations: sorcery, divination, witchcraft, mediums, and psychics (spiritualists). The man of God warned him of impending judgment, but he ignored the warnings. Judgment struck in a humiliating manner, bringing loss and shame. Then Manasseh finally repented, but it was too late. (2 Chronicles 33:1-13)

In the 1960s, during the Jesus Movement, another group arose calling themselves "The Children of God." This cultish group formed communes they called "colonies." They spoke of their love for Jesus, yet among their teachings existed some blatantly perverse ideas about worship and evangelism.

In 1974 The Children of God launched a new method of so-called evangelism called, *"Flirty Fishing"* - using sex to win converts and support. The *intention* of "flirty fishing" was to win male converts to the group. The girls would go out, meet men, and engage in sex with them. This was all done with the *intention* of "evangelizing" these male victims and bringing them into the cult.

Founder David Berg wrote in 1973, *"We have a sexy God and a sexy religion with a very sexy leader with an extremely sexy young following!"*[122]

A female ex-member said, "We were supposed to be God's whores."[123]

You could say the *intention* of evangelism was "good," but the method was a clear biblical violation. As always, embarrassing judgment eventually catches up with those who mix God with forbidden practices. Hard times fell upon these people when the cult was publicly exposed for incest and child sex abuse. All the allegations of sexual abuse finally came into the light concerning founder, David Berg. Interpol launched an investigation into Berg's activities and the FBI was investigating him as well. Berg fled to Portugal in 1993, where he died the next year.[124]

INTENTION OF GOING TO "A BETTER PLACE"

I wonder how many people pass through this life on earth with the *intention* of going to heaven, only to awake in the regions of the damned?

Many of my readers will remember that March day in 1997 when police found the bodies of 39 members of a San Diego cult, Heaven's Gate, who had committed mass suicide with the *intention* of meeting up with a spaceship flying behind the passing Hale-Bopp comet that would transport them into heaven.[125]

"What we're finding is that each and every one of the members of the organization, prior to their death, gave a brief statement ... The essence of those statements were that **they were going to a better place**," Jerry Lipscomb of the San Diego Sheriff's Department said.[126]

Intention matters very little if the action is wrong. If someone *intended* to show you how a handgun worked and accidentally shot you in the process, you would still suffer the consequences regardless of the original intention.

NURSE GIVES UP YOGA AFTER 19 YEARS

Janet Munday, BSN, RN, who serves as the Mid-Atlantic Regional Director of the National Association of Catholic Nurses, U.S.A., practiced yoga for 19 years before realizing that she could no longer do so and maintain her faith. Though her *intention* was to establish a stronger connection with the Holy Spirit, she found herself deceived, turning inward, and being led away from the Savior.

"Yoga exercise did not lead me toward stronger connections with God. It deceived me in using meditations to turn inward on myself instead of linking me with the Holy Spirit. It may have provided me increased flexibility and strength while it blindly weakened my relationship to the Trinity...I have been enlightened and am a witness for Christ." [127]

According to *The Christian Post*, Pastor Mark Driscoll said, "If you just sign up for a little yoga class, you're signing up for a little demon class...that's what you are doing. And Satan doesn't care if you stretch as long as you go to hell."[128]

While others are enthusiastically joining Christian Yoga groups, today more and more Christians are discerning the real spirit behind yoga and abandoning the postures. Dr. Laurette Willis, founder of "Praise Moves" spent 22 years of her life in yoga. Yoga led Laurette Willis into a New Age lifestyle.[129]

Now she's warning others of the spiritual pitfalls—and offering an alternative. She gave her life to Jesus Christ and never went back to yoga. She published an article recently entitled, **12 Reasons Why Yoga is NOT Good for Christians.** If someone you love and care about is doing yoga—even so-called Christian Yoga—you may want to share Laurette's article with them.[130] You can find it at PraiseMoves.com

There are clearly some sincere people who *believe* they're much closer to God because of their "Christian Yoga" class. These are not wicked or perverse people. They're not trying to weasel you out of money, or to bring a curse on their fellow yogis.

However, if we really listen to what is said in the Christian brands of yoga, and carefully examine the content, you'll notice a mystical, feeling-based version of Christianity that cannot possibly co-exist in true Bible believers. The people participating in some brand of Christian Yoga seem to believe that their feelings supersede the Bible, even though they would never actually vocalize that.

Again, let me say, God gave us His Holy Word and His Holy Spirit; He never gave us holy yoga.[131]

If you are a Spirit-filled believer, you possess a heavenly creative power. It's already in you (Ephesians 3:20). If you would sincerely seek the Lord Jesus Christ, I wouldn't be surprised if the Holy Spirit would give you some real heavenly exercise postures that glorified Jesus, instead of using stolen postures from an old polytheistic religion.

Then as you authentically honored the Lord, maybe He'd show you how to go global with your new Christ-honoring exercise moves, and maybe He'd even show you how to begin a powerful international franchise that would bring all kinds of influence and resources to you for the Great Commission, the poor, charity, and for your family's future.

It's difficult to imagine why a Spirit-filled believer would pirate exercise postures from the Hindu religion and then try to incorporate them into their Christian practices. Our God is creative and generous, so willing to give His sincere seekers fresh knowledge, wisdom, and revelation that will not cover their identity or hold back their real destiny. If you've ever visited India, then you would know that a system that never worked for the Indian people will certainly never work in a positive way for God's people.

God will impart His glory, His holiness, and His anointing to those who refuse to yoke with foreign deities and who show that they really love God with all their heart, soul, and strength.

Romans 9:23-24 (TPT)
[23] And doesn't he also have the right to release the revelation of the wealth of his glory to his vessels of mercy, whom God prepared beforehand to receive his glory?

[24] Even for us, whether we are Jews or non-Jews, we are those he has called to experience his glory.

2 Corinthians 3:18 (TPT)
...with no veil we all become like mirrors who brightly reflect the glory of the Lord Jesus. We are being transfigured into his very image as we move from one brighter level of glory to another. And this glorious transfiguration comes from the Lord, who is the Spirit.

Ephesians 3:16 (TPT)
[16] And I pray that he would unveil within you the unlimited riches of his glory and favor until supernatural strength floods your innermost being with his divine might and explosive power.

Some enjoy the pride of being part of a trendy, worldly, religious exercise, without considering the dangers to their spiritual life down the road. My prayer is that you will develop into an authentic glory-bearer of the risen Son of God, Jesus Christ, walking in truth, being protected by God and walking in the manifest presence of the Holy Spirit.

Now, we're going to explore the most dangerous moment in a person's life.

11

LOSING THE ABILITY TO DISCERN THE TRUTH

The Most Dangerous Moment in Your Life

*But I fear that somehow, as the serpent deceived
Eve through his trickery, so your minds might be
led astray from the simplicity that is in Christ.*
~ *2 Corinthians 11:3 MEV*

The yoga world was shaken when William J. Broad's article, "Yoga and Sex Scandals: No Surprise Here," was published in the New York Times.[132]

He wrote, "Yoga teachers and how-to books seldom mention that the discipline began as a sex cult." Broad writes that Hatha Yoga began as a branch of Tantra and could include group and individual sex in its rites.

We'll get back to this later, but let's first look at why certain people join yoga groups today. Certainly sincere believers don't enroll in Christian Yoga sessions with the fantasy of participating in illicit individual or group sex. So what's the attraction?

Our human tendency is to want to fit in with those around us and to be accepted into certain clubs, organizations, and persuasions. We want to belong to something popular.

Satan is very aware of this tendency, so in order to change deep-rooted beliefs or opinions such as biblical convictions, the devil has developed a clever strategy. He knows he can succeed in his seduction if he can ease you into a forbidden practice with baby steps. He entices target victims by using others who have already accepted, adopted, and are practicing a falsehood.

The first step Satan takes in his plan is to present common ground—something with which you can generally agree. For example, exercise, health, and stress relief are things most everyone acknowledges are good things. Who wouldn't agree? Yet, once the common ground is established, it becomes notably easier for him to gradually introduce contradictory ideas that casually and progressively draw you away from the faith in which you were previously rooted.

Years ago I read a book by George Barna called *The Frog in the Kettle*.[133] Barna provided an important illustration on how perversions and aberrations that used to shock us, no longer do so because little by little we become desensitized. For example, a frog will immediately jump out of a boiling pot of water. However, if the frog is placed in cool, comfortable water in a kettle, and the heat is incrementally increased, the frog will stay in the kettle until it is too late and the water is boiling him to death. It reminds us of something Solomon said:

Proverbs 29:1 (MSG)
For people who hate discipline and only get more stubborn, there'll come a day when life tumbles in and they break, but by then it'll be too late to help them.

And Hosea, the prophet also warned about a time when it's too late to repent.

Hosea 5:6 (MSG)
When they decide to get their lives together and go off looking for God once again, they'll find it's too late.

Could the frog in the kettle illustrate how modern yoga entices Christians to join in the pagan poses?

1. First, you want to be trendy, and yoga certainly is trendy and in vogue.

2. Second, you desire to be accepted by a group, and the non-judgmental yoginis in the group accept you joyfully, making you feel so special.

3. Third, you agree this practice really is good for you physically and mentally.[134]

4. Fourth, without notice, you begin receiving small spiritual deceptions which eventually open you up to greater deceptions.

5. Fifth, you begin to question some of your original beliefs about Christ and replace them with the concepts unqualified teachers have told you.

6. Sixth, you begin to lose your spiritual discernment.

7. Seventh, you start rejecting the people who really care about you because they are concerned about your practices and what they are doing to you spiritually.

8. Eighth, you begin to prioritize other types of events rather than those involving genuine, spiritual worship of the One True God.

I won't go on, but you can see the progression. Anyone who has received Christ's deliverance from the yoga cult, when their spiritual eyes were opened, immediately saw the step-by-step regression from Christ while progressing more deeply into yogic doctrines of sorcery.

When yoga adherents reach stage six, losing spiritual discernment, they have entered the most dangerous moment of their lives.

LOSING THE ABILITY TO DISCERN

What if you were flying somewhere and the airline told you they just made some maintenance repairs on the aircraft? Mechanics weren't able to find authorized parts so they used some parts from an old automobile. Then they told you there is one chance in ten the plane will crash? Would you get on board? What if they said there's only one chance in 100 that the plane will crash. Would you board the plane?

What if practicing yoga poses gave you one chance in ten of picking up a demon? Would you practice it? What if you knew there was one chance in 100 that you would attract a demon to your life and your family? Would you perform the poses? I'm not suggesting that a Christian will become demon-possessed, but they can certainly acquire a demonic "cling-on" that will lure them into deeper realms of spiritual darkness and bring serious consequences to their lives and families.

It baffles me as to why Christians would lug doctrines of demons from other religions into their Christian practices.

In 1980, while I was in Orchard Park, New York, I met Dr David Cho, pastor of the world's largest church. At that time, his church enjoyed 50,000 members. Thirty years later, his church in South Korea enjoyed 800,000 members. Dr. Cho taught us an unusual "secret" God had revealed to him as he studied the Bible. He taught that part of our faith walk involved envisioning things, not as they are but as they should be. It was something Dr. Cho called, *The Fourth Dimension.*[135]

It was a new teaching to many, and some labeled Dr. Cho as a "heretic." He talked about vision, faith, calling things that are not as though they were, and meditation. In his teaching, he continually led us to God's Word, the Bible, to show examples of these practices; nonetheless, he caught a lot of criticism from the so-called "discernment groups." Dr. Cho showed us how using God's Word and envisioning by faith, we could experience great, and miraculous results in our lives. He cited many biblical examples.

Cho offered a clear biblical basis for his teaching, even though it seemed new to many of his listeners. He was

Bible-based. But there is nothing biblical about yoga. Nothing at all. You have to change, distort or twist God's Word to get any Bible-believer to even consider yoga as a Christian practice.

Christian brands of yoga were pirated from Hinduism and syncretized into a so-called Christian practice, making it not truly Christian at all. There is absolutely nothing biblical about the practice, although some teachers try to convince you with twisted and misquoted Scriptures.

Corinna Craft, the former yoga instructor, gave a forceful warning about how trying to merge Christian spirituality with yoga opens you up to Hindu spirits.[136]

Without discernment, your divine defenses are inactive, and you may be naively opening your life, your family, and your future to the demonic realm.

In the next chapter, we'll study some of the yoga poses and what they really mean.

12

THE POSES OF YOGA: A SEXUAL SYSTEM?

Did Yoga Really Begin as a Sex Cult?
For all that is in the world—the lust of the flesh, the lust of the eyes, and the pride of life—is not of the Father, but is of the world.
~ 1 John 2:16 MEV

Most Christian Yoga classes practice Hatha Yoga. Many times the poses are actually depictions of Hindu gods, unbeknownst to the beginner. Hatha Yoga classes in America and the Western World often use innocuous English terms instead of the Eastern terms used in the yogic practice. For example, they may teach you about breathing procedures, techniques, or approaches instead of "pranayama." Similarly, they may teach about energy centers (or points) instead of "chakras," mindfulness (or centering) rather than meditation, and poses (or postures) instead of "asanas."[137]

Now, let's begin looking at the poses of yoga. Sometimes you'll hear the term "asana" used instead of poses or postures. Asanas are the Sanskrit names for yoga poses (or postures). "Asana" is defined as any of the yogic postures or movements.

1. Sun Salutation: Greeting the Hindu Sun god, Surya

This posture is often one of the first series of poses done directly after seated breathing exercises during morning yoga sessions.

This salutation has twelve distinct poses; each designed to greet the sun as a way to worship the Hindu sun god, Surya.

2. Downward Facing Dog Pose: Positioning your Spirit

This is a combined stretch in which you turn inward simultaneously connecting to your center while stretching your body into a long line.

This pose is meant to *position your spirit* within while staying connected to the outside world.

3. Lotus Pose: A Sexual/Spiritual Event?

This pose is for the purpose of opening yourself up for a spirit to come into you or upon you. It is usually depicting a sexual act. You sit crossing your legs with your fingers touching your thumbs.

According to the Christian Truth Center, something supposedly arrives in the spirit realm known as the "diamond." The "diamond" is said to be like a phallus (penis) that approaches and then enters you. *"The lotus position forms a spiritual penis and it enters you and performs sexual acts with you. You cannot refuse it so it just comes and enters you."* [138]

Is it any wonder there are so many sex scandals in the yoga world? Just go to your search engine and type in "yoga sex scandals" and watch page-after-page of stories and news items about this subject. I'm not saying there aren't sex scandals in other realms, even in Christianity. But it seems that yoga fosters or attracts a lustful spirit which could make it easier for unintended "encounters" to occur.

In fact, a life-long missionary in India noticed a connection between yoga and lust.

A MISSIONARY HERO'S ASSESSMENT OF YOGA

The late Alfred Cawston founded the Southern Asia Bible College in 1951 situated in the city of Bangalore, India. He and his wife Elizabeth had been missionaries in India for thirty years. The impact of the work they did had been felt in many parts of the world, and still today the Southern Asia Bible College is one of the largest Bible Colleges and Christian training centers in all of Asia. [139]

Our friend, Patty Booher met Alfred while she was attending Central Bible College. Alfred was serving as a Missionary in Residence at the Bible College. He made an indelible imprint on Patty's life upon which she often reflects, and even included him in her book *Reflections of a Wyoming Shepherd on the 23rd Psalm,*[140] relating the supernatural impact he had on her life. Alfred and his

125

wife, Elizabeth became wonderful friends with the Booher family over the years.

Patty remembers, "When Alfred and Elizabeth came to our home, they just melted into the scene, taking the children on their laps and loving each of us."

"I still try to tell Christians what Alfred told me about yoga," Patty continues, "But if they have been involved for very long, they just blow it off. Nonetheless, I firmly believe he was 'spot on' in his assessment of yoga.

"Let me explain.

"The first time Alfred came to visit us, we were pastoring in Wichita, Kansas. My daughter was just a tiny baby at that time. My husband and I needed to go to the store, so Alfred said, 'Just leave the baby with me.' So we did.

"When we returned home, Alfred seemed greatly disturbed or distressed about something. What was it?

"He had picked up the Sunday newspaper and the special weekend entertainment portion was tucked inside. He looked at the back page and found a full-page ad for yoga books.

"He looked at us with a sad concern and said, 'I am deeply grieved for America. I watched this yoga practice in India for many years. Once it comes, you cannot stop it. It is disguised as exercise, but that is a lie. As you draw deeper into the exercise, you become amazed at what your body can do. But **they don't realize it is all centered around an evil spirit, and with that spirit comes many other spirits such as the demon behind pornography.**'

"It has been 47 years since that conversation with Alfred

and because I knew this man as a man after God's own heart. I trusted what he said."

I believe Alfred Cawston's spiritual discernment was absolutely correct.

Patty's book, *Reflections of a Wyoming Shepherd on the 23rd Psalm*[141] is still available.

Before we get to the spiritual meaning of more of the yoga poses, let me simply give you a list of some headlines I found concerning yoga and sex scandals. You can read them if you wish; I have put the reference locations in my endnotes. Or you are welcome to skip over them by simply reading the headlines.

THE HEADLINES:

1. The Dark Side of Yoga[142]

2. Update: Yoga Scandals and Sex Cults[143] (from *The Wild Hunt,* a pagan news and commentary site that admits yoga and Wicca have the same core roots.)

3. Pasadena Yoga Instructor Convicted of Sexual Battery[144]

4. A List of Yoga Scandals Involving Gurus, Teachers, Students, Sex and Other Inappropriate Behavior[145]

5. Twisted relationships: Inside yoga sex scandals[146]

6. Yoga and Sex[147]

7. Why So Many Yoga Sex Scandals?[148]

8. He Said He Could Do What He Wanted': The Scandal That Rocked Bikram Yoga[149]

9. Update: Yoga Scandals and Sex Cults[150]

10. Scandal-Ridden Yoga Movement Struggles to Embrace #MeToo Despite Starting As A Sex Cult[151]

11. Yoga Massage Scandals and Yoga Sex Scandals: A Response from Yogi Dashama[152]

12. Sex Scandal for Yoga Guru![153]

13. Swami Nithyananda Sex Scandal Videos— Lessons to Learn [154]

14. Satyananda Yoga Reeling from Horrific Details of Sex Abuse, Rape Allegations and Accountability[155]

15. Australia's Underage Yoga Sex Cult: The Survivors Speak Out[156]

16. Sex Scandal Rocks Yoga World[157]

17. Sexual Abuse in Yoga—the Secret We Can't Ignore[158]

18. The Mysterious Death of a Tantric Sex Guru[159]

19. Yoga and Sex Scandals: No Surprise Here[160]

20. Yoga unmasked as pagan sex cult[161]

21. "Dallas woman says she was forced out of faith-based Holy Yoga for reporting sexual harassment during class"[162]

I think you get the point. Now let's get back to the spiritual meaning of the yoga poses. We've already briefly looked at the first three: the sun salutation, the downward facing dog pose, and the sexually charged lotus pose. Now let's talk about seven more yoga poses and what they mean.

4. Headstand Poses: Inviting Kundalini, the Counterfeit Holy Spirit

These headstand poses are some of the most "spiritually impacting yoga poses." These poses are to awaken the serpent energy in the base of the spine bringing it to the crown of the head.

Some yogis claim you can achieve an enlightened mind and fresh boldness after receiving the "kundalini awakening." Christian apologists and discerners often call the kundalini spirit "the counterfeit Holy Spirit" because unwise and undiscerning Christians actually believe they are having an encounter with the Holy Spirit.

I know I repeat myself, but this is something enormously important to remember, especially in these days of high deception. Here it is: Discernment is our lifeline!

5. Animal Poses

There are a variety of animal poses in yoga. Lion pose, cobra pose, cat pose, eagle pose, etc. The purpose of each animal pose is to incite you to possess the attributes of that animal.

For example, the eagle pose is said to bring you a clear "mind's eye." The lion pose is to attract bravery and control. The cobra pose looks like a snake rearing its head saying, "Don't mess with me."

6. Strength Poses

These postures are alleged to help you attract power from the Hindu deities and make you feel stronger.

7. Ananta Asana

This is a reclined pose said to relieve fatigue.

In this pose, your body reclines on one side, and your top leg is lifted and held with your arm. Sometimes this is referred to as the "hand-to-big-toe pose."

The name for this posture comes from the Indian Sanskrit and is named after "Ananta," the serpent with 1,000 heads. Asana simply means pose; thus, the name Ananta Asana, often spelled "Anantasana."[163]

8. Danda Asana

Danda Asana is named after the staff carried by those who have achieved the title of "Swami Danda." The swami's staff is said to represent the spinal column and forms the path for the energy of self-awakening. Danda Asana is considered to be a perfect pose for supporting a practitioner's spiritual journey.[164]

9. Warrior Pose

The multiple forms of warrior pose (there are three main poses and three other variations) are all derived from the ancient story of a warrior named Virabhadra, the son of Hindu god Shiva.[165]

10. Tree Pose

The origins of this pose come from an Indian epic poem by Ramayana. In part of the poem, a woman named Sita is captured by the demon king Ravana, who holds her prisoner and tries to convince her to forget about her husband, Rama. Convinced that Rama will come save her, Sita finds peace among the trees outside the palace where she meditates and waits for Rama to rescue her.[166]

11. Corpse Pose

The corpse pose is usually the last pose in a yoga session. It is performed while lying on your back on your mat. The intention of this pose is to mimic death to help you prepare for it.

The Christian Research Network published a warning to churches that promote yoga and so-called Christian Yoga. Apologist Chris Lawson urges pastors to know the truth about yoga. He explains how the poses, the breathing techniques, and meditations are all based on the occult philosophy of Eastern mystical systems.

"Eastern occult spirituality is being embraced by many who call themselves Christians, under the guise of 'Christian Yoga exercise.'"[167]

Today we are even learning of scientists warning about yoga being "more dangerous than previously thought."[168]

Christian Ministries International is now sending out a heartfelt cry to Christians everywhere.

"If you're a Christian who has mistakenly gotten involved in the practice of yoga, we strongly encourage you to stop now. There is no excuse for staying involved in a pagan religious activity created to tap into demonic spiritual forces." [169]

BRINGING DEMONIC ENTITIES INTO YOUR HOME

My publisher (*Hope in the Last Days*), Charisma Media, ran a web piece by a former witch and yogini who met Jesus Christ. She warns Christians of the spiritual dangers of yoga and the connection it holds with Satan, himself.[170]

Beth Eckert, a former witch turned Christian writes, "People might assume that yoga will provide the body with several health benefits," but she warns that "doing these Eastern spiritual practices will only do otherwise. By aligning the body with the kingdom of darkness people are inviting the devil to cause great harm to one's physical and spiritual wellbeing." She reports, "Once you bring these practices into your life, you are also inviting these demonic entities into your home and your family."[171]

Jessica Smith, author of *The Shattering—An Encounter with Truth*, was a certified yoga instructor and master level Reiki practitioner when the lens through which she viewed the world was shattered in a moment with a profound experience that revealed to her the dark spiritual reality behind these practices. It is now her goal to share the truth behind these poses and exercises.[172]

She writes concerning the poses of yoga, "Did you know yoga is not a series of stretches? It is actually an ancient religion with its own god, practices, and doctrine. The poses and breathing are only one aspect of the religion. These components have only recently become popularized, but the religion of yoga has been practiced for thousands of years."[173]

With all the former yoga practitioners that have left the

practice for Jesus, it's difficult to understand why Christians are now running to and joining these Christian Yoga groups. It's mind-boggling to even think that genuine believers, after all the warnings issued by respected Christian leaders and sincere apologists, would continue in this ancient occult practice.

"...with straight faces all of the yogis insist that practicing yoga will not change anyone's religious beliefs. This is the religion of Antichrist; and for the first time in history it is being widely practiced throughout the Western world." [174] (Hunt, Dave and McMayhon, T.A., The Seduction of Christianity – Spiritual Discernment in the Last Days, p.54, Harvest House Publishers, Eugene, Oregon 97402)

And with sincere expressions they also tell you that randomly-controlled scientific studies on the effects of yoga show great physical and mental benefits. But...at the cost of your soul? Even ten thousand scientific studies can never cleanse an occult practice of its dark spiritual dimensions.

CHRISTIAN ASSEMBLIES INTERNATIONAL ISSUES SERIOUS YOGA WARNING

And now, *Christian Assemblies International* has published a warning to Christians about the spiritual deception of yoga.[175]

The actual physical poses of yoga have serious occult implications and seem to trigger certain types of demonic reactions the practitioners misunderstand to be some kind of spiritual "awakening."

I pray that Church leaders globally will take the spiritual origins of the yoga poses seriously. If they do, they will have great success in reaching those involved in the New

Age Movement and yoga. If they don't, we could lose a generation of souls affected by the hidden spirits behind yoga and other New Age practices.

The real question now is: Do you want to follow Shiva, the Lord of Yoga who is also named "the Destroyer" or do you want to follow Jesus Christ, the Lord of Lords in whom is life and the light of men (John 1:4). It's your choice.

13

THE DECEPTION OF YOGA

Transitioning into Darkness?

...beware lest you also fall from your own firm footing, being led away by the deception of the wicked.
~ 2 Peter 3:17 MEV

Does yoga facilitate a deceptive spiritual environment? Those of you who sincerely desire the truth about yoga are reading these words now. Those who have bitten into the seducer's bait; those who have already transitioned into the darkness of deception, won't read the truth or listen to the truth. In fact, they'll probably brag about reading a few paragraphs and tossing this "pharisaical nonsense" aside, refusing to read further. And their words will probably project an arrogant and cleverly sarcastic tone.

Those who have already determined to enthusiastically follow a hypocritical falsehood probably won't read the truth from reliable and honest ministers or friends who really care about them. Intercessory prayer for their souls is critical. You, who know the truth of God's Word, His nature, His character, His commandments, and His will, must engage the realm of God's Spirit, praying for their release from the lies that are erecting substantial strongholds in their souls.

1 Timothy 4:1 (TPT)
The Holy Spirit has explicitly revealed: At the end of this age, many will depart from the true faith one after another, devoting themselves to spirits of deception and following demon-inspired revelations and theories.

YOGA FEATURED AT CHRISTIAN WOMEN'S CONFERENCE

According to the Christian News Network (August 22, 2018), a women's conference at a large Texas church featured a yoga session. An instructor from a yoga studio in Dallas led a session at the event. According to the instructor's social media post, she led the women in a "yoga session where we focused on: physical wellness with strength, flexibility, mobility, and balance; mental wellness by reciting positive affirmations and being mindful of our thoughts regarding ourselves (mindfulness); emotional wellness by focusing on conscious breathing, and letting go!" [176]

What followed next was perhaps a well-deserved furious storm of reaction. One social media commenter wrote, *"This is very dangerous practice to introduce in the church. It may seem innocent, but it really isn't. Who will stop people from going into deeper forms of yoga?"*

Another wrote, *"When one opens up their spirit, the enemy has the legal right to bring all kinds of corruption to one's soul. I have cast out many demons that have entered in this fashion. This is not right."*

"Is Heaven so bankrupt that you have to borrow from the devil?" another inquired.

Another wrote, *"Please research before you lead these beautiful ladies to worship that's not of God."*

The yoga instructor parroted some of the phrases I've heard or read over and over again from both New Age and Christian-brand Yoga instructors alike. Phrases similar to these:

"Yoga does not belong to one religion."

"Yoga is neutral."

"Yoga is just a great exercise."

"Set your own intention for yoga."

"Yoga predates Hinduism."

"Yoga has a scientific backing."

"Yoga, like God, is too big to be confined to any one faith."

"Yoga tunes your body, which is the temple of God."

"The perfect person sees nothing but God in yoga."

"Yoga is spiritual but not religious."

"Yoga helps you deepen your faith and connects you with Christ."

WORN-OUT DISTORTIONS OF THE TRUTH

These are the same old, worn-out distortions of the truth, recited over and over again. Sadly, some professing Christians have bought into the deception. In one way or another, you can anticipate hearing these familiar tunes, or similar clichés, from every New Age or Christian Yoga teacher you may encounter. When you meet the victims that have joined any of the Christian brands of yoga, you'll hear them all echoing the same cleverly-designed, justifying distortions which really are "as fragile as clay pots."

Job 13:12 (NLT)
Your platitudes are as valuable as ashes. Your defense is as fragile as a clay pot.

According to a professor at Michigan State University, if you get on board with a yoga class that's labeled and marketed as "Hot," "New Age," or any other trendy type of American yoga, you're supporting and promoting a business model based on theft.[177] This would include all the Christian Yoga brands.

Exodus 20:15 (NLT)
"You must not steal."

Ephesians 4:28 (NLT)
If you are a thief, quit stealing.

Romans 2:21 (NLT)
Well then, if you teach others, why don't you teach yourself? You tell others not to steal, but do you steal?

DO CHRISTIAN YOGA MARKETERS TELL THE TRUTH?

Why can't they just tell the unvarnished truth? Why do these yoga teachers cloak the truth about yoga with slogans, half-truths, and biblical misrepresentations?

Habakkuk 1:8b (NLT)
Like eagles, they swoop down to devour their prey.

I'm telling the truth and am labeled a "nitpicker." If you've known me for any length of time, you know I am actually an embracing believer, far from being a nitpicker. I love all of God's people. I've never been quick to judge others based on peripheral, non-essential matters.

UNDERMINING THE NATURE OF JESUS CHRIST

Yet, when something comes along *undermining the very nature* of Jesus Christ as the Truth, it is no frivolous or petty matter. If I didn't believe people's souls and families were at stake, I wouldn't bother doing hundreds of hours of research and writing. I'm doing it so you will know the truth.

John 8:32 (NLT)
"And you will know the truth, and the truth will set you free."

Twenty-eight times in the Gospel according to Matthew, Jesus used the phrase, "I tell you the truth." It would seem that His sincere followers would take note and tell the truth ... about yoga. In John's Gospel account, Jesus said, "I am the Truth."

St. Paul addressed the problem with immature, undiscerning Christians in the first century. Some were accepting "new teachings" and "lies so clever they sounded like the truth."

Ephesians 4:14 (NLT)
We will no longer be immature like children. We won't be tossed and blown about by every wind of new teaching. *We will not be influenced when people try to trick us with lies so clever they sound like the truth.* (emphasis mine)

The late Ray Yungen, who had studied religious movements for decades, wrote the book, *Yoga: Exercise or Religion—Does it Matter?* In it, he outlined that "while many view yoga as harmless exercise, there is no denying that the practice is rooted in Eastern New Age religion."[178]

FALLING PREY TO DANGEROUS IDEAS

Ray continued, "**Believers in Christ have fallen** prey to some dangerous ideas. One is that we feel free to draw from pagan sources. Or, as is popularly stated, we can 'chew the meat and spit out the bones.' But this doesn't make any sense from a biblical standpoint. As a Christian, we can't segregate into portions what part we think will do us harm and what part will profit us. If the foundational spirituality is contrary to God's Word, then it will be folly to interact with it."

Bob Larson, a well-known Christian deliverance minister and dependable authority on cults and the occult wrote *Larson's New Book of Cults*[179] and *Larson's Book of World Religions and Alternative Spirituality*.[180] Both books contain chapters on yoga. Larson is affectionately known as the "real exorcist" because he really does cast real demons out of people in his meetings, just the way Jesus did in His earthly ministry. And he's cast out hundreds of "yoga demons" from yoga devotees who never dreamed they could ever attract such an entity.

Bob wrote, "Quite literally, yoga's goal is to tune the body to the universal mind and thereby achieve god-consciousness and attain oneness with the universe. At least that's what they've been doing for thousands of years in India, no matter what some ignorant Christians in American may call their brand of holy yoga."[181]

SERIOUS WARNING TO CHRISTIANS

Bob warns Christians to stay far away from any format of yoga including the "so-called Christian transmutations."[182]

Bob Larson has had to deal with the collateral damage in people's lives that got involved in Christian Yoga and later came for deliverance.

In his book, Bob says, "The postures are designed to condition the mind to experience altered states of consciousness. Each pose is presumed to be tuning the body, glands, and psychic nervous system to a level of spiritual susceptibility and altered awareness."

Bob lamented, "Almost every week, I pick up the spiritual

collateral damage of those who got sucked in to this lie of 'Christian' yoga and became demonized. I know of no legitimate exorcist or deliverance minister who approves of such nonsense." [183]

He explains, "They evoke the yogic god within, align their chakras, and awaken the Kundalini power at the base of the spine. **And they get demons."**

SATAN'S TACTICS

One of Satan's tactics is first, to deceive the devotee, and second, prepare him or her as fertile ground for actual demonization (accepting "clip-on" demons, meaning those that attach themselves to your life). Next, the devotee is remodeled into a clever, subtle salesperson for the devil himself, motivating others to step into the same snare. It's hard to believe, but Christians, once solid, are now becoming missionaries for Hindu gods through various brands of yoga.

THE HOLY SPIRIT SPEAKS TO THOSE WHO RESPOND TO HIM

I have a friend who is a board member of Strategic Global Mission, my ministry.[184] Judy O'Leary is a well-educated, certified strength and conditioning coach, and co-author of the popular book *Upward*.[185]

When Judy was just a new Christian, her boss wanted her to offer yoga classes at the fitness gym. So, thinking yoga was merely stretching exercises, she innocently ordered videos on yoga poses and read all she could about the "science of yoga." She diligently studied and practiced Hatha Yoga, and was determined to leave out the meditations and "Om's" or "Aum's" (Om in yoga is the "basic sound of the universe and chanting it symbolically and physically tunes the yogi into that sound and acknowledges their connection to everything in the world and the universe"). Judy determined to not present any spiritual connection to yoga's real roots of ancient Shamanism or Hinduism.

As expected, many women signed up for the sessions. Judy led them in the yoga postures, but only as an exercise. After several sessions, however, she noticed the students were curiously changing. "They started developing a certain culture," Judy noticed. "Some even began to bow to me with folded hands. And I noticed that others were plunging into deeper forms of yoga and their personalities were transmuting, as if something was taking them over."

What Judy didn't know at that time is that Hatha Yoga was specifically designed to lead the practitioner into deeper yogic realms. Former yoga guru, Marilyn Ferguson describes it as a "devilish trap" that opens your appetite for the occult.[186]

The deception that Hatha Yoga is 'purely physical' is a gross distortion of the truth and begs the question: 'Why the cover up?' The Truth never leads anyone into an occult practice, so the marketers must have realized that they had to present yoga as something it's not.

"Then the Holy Spirit spoke to me," Judy continued. "I was just a brand-new Christian at the time, but I heard Him say, 'Judy, get out. Don't teach this anymore!' So, I went to my boss and said, 'I cannot teach yoga anymore.' He protested, 'But it's bringing in more money than anything else here.'"

Nonetheless, Judy was resolute in her decision and never taught yoga again. And God has blessed her today beyond her wildest dreams. There's something about doing the will of God that brings mammoth benefits and advantages to your life. Equally true, there's something about doing what is not the will of God that brings complications and disfavor to our lives.

Many years later, Judy heard about something called "Holy Yoga" that certain women were trying to bring into the church. Church leaders asked if she'd be willing to check it out to see if it was legitimately a holy practice. Once again, the Holy Spirit nudged her heart with a loving whisper, "Don't go. Have no part in it, not even to investigate." She immediately responded to the Holy Spirit's nudge, and once again the Lord lavished her with many unusual blessings, strategic opportunities, and supernatural favor.

The question now is this: If God would speak to Judy, why wouldn't He speak to other Christians who have become involved in yoga?

My answer is: I believe God has spoken to them. I believe the Holy Spirit is always faithful to warn us of dangers. The problem is not that God doesn't warn, but that people don't respond to those warnings. Some once fruitful believers ignored the voice of the Holy Spirit, became trapped in a deception, and now focus primarily on temporal things instead of eternal matters.

Do you believe Christians are free to "connect with God" in whatever way they choose?

14

CHAPTER

ARE WE FREE TO CONNECT WITH GOD OUR OWN WAY?

Authentic Liberty and Freedom Are Found in a Person, Not in a System

There is one God, and one mediator between God and men, the Man Christ Jesus.
~ 1 Timothy 2:5

A Hindu says, "Hinduism gives us the freedom to approach God in our own way without demanding conformity to any dogma."[187]

This sounds a lot like some of the Christian Yoga promoters today. "You can approach God and connect to Christ with yoga ... if you determine your own intention."

While we do enjoy a new liberty in the Lord Jesus,[188]

147

God's Word gives us no such freedom to approach God in any way we desire. There is only one way to connect with God and only one mediator between God and man. Just before teaching about His coming judgment on false prophets and teachers, Jesus described the difference between those who believe they can approach God their own way and those who choose to connect with God *His* way.

Matthew 7:13-14 (NASB)

[13] "Enter through the narrow gate; for the gate is wide and the way is broad that leads to destruction, and there are many who enter through it.

[14] For the gate is small and the way is narrow that leads to life, and there are few who find it.

Authentic liberty and freedom are found in a Person, not in a system.

John 14:6 (NKJV)

Jesus said to him, "I am the way, the truth, and the life. No one comes to the Father except through Me.

1 Timothy 2:5 (NKJV)

[5] For there is one God and one Mediator between God and men, the Man Christ Jesus

When you start hearing about "chakras," "kundalini," "energy points," "pranayama," and "eight limbs of yoga" in your yoga class, you have identified the hidden Hindu teachings from the Indian Sanskrit. I would run as fast as I could if I heard any of these subjects taught anywhere!

1 Corinthians 10:14 (NLT)
So, my dear friends, flee from the worship of idols.

WHY DO THEY TALK MORE ABOUT YOGA THAN THEY DO ABOUT JESUS?

I have searched but not been able to find a book on yoga, including Christian Yoga that does not incorporate the spiritual concepts found in classic Hinduism. They almost always speak of *"The Yoga Sutras of Patañjali,"* the notable scholar of the Samkhya school of Hindu philosophy.

The "Christian" Yoga books and blogs I've read, and the videos I've reviewed seem to be more about Hindu philosophies than Jesus Christ and God's Word, yet these Christian-brand Yoga promoters claim to be "preachers of the Gospel."[189]

I have yet to find the *pure Gospel and unadulterated* Word of God in any literature from the Christian Yoga brands. Who trained and ordained these self-proclaimed "preachers of the Gospel?"

Why do they talk more about yoga than they do about Jesus? Why can I not find a clear presentation of the Gospel of Jesus Christ in Christian Yoga brands? It's because you cannot separate yoga into physical and spiritual parts. And you cannot syncretize the Gospel with yoga philosophies. Yoga is physical, but it's also spiritual. And spiritual does not mean biblical or the Gospel. Remember, Satan himself is very spiritual. Once again, I quote the Apostle Paul:

2 Corinthians 11:13-15 (KJV)
[13] For such are false apostles, deceitful workers,

149

> transforming themselves into the apostles of Christ.
>
> [14] And no marvel; for Satan himself is transformed into an angel of light.
>
> [15] Therefore it is no great thing if his ministers also be transformed as the ministers of righteousness; whose end shall be according to their works.

I recently read an article entitled, "Christ Consciousness: Why You Have the Same Capabilities as Jesus." It tells how Jesus attained "Christ consciousness" and how you can too, and actually receive the same capabilities as Jesus once had, and you can do it through yoga. Not through the Holy Spirit and faith in God's Word, but through yoga, you can do the same miracles Jesus did, the writer asserts.

The article continues by talking about how yoga helps you reach the level of "Christ consciousness."[190]

IS YOGA PART OF THE OCCULT?

Bible Theology Ministries of Wales and the United Kingdom sums it up succinctly:

"Yoga is a part of the occult. It is not possible to separate yoga from occultism and it is not possible for Christians to do yoga exercises with impunity. Note that Shiva, one of Hinduism's most powerful gods, known as 'the destroyer,' is named 'Yogi Swara' ... 'Lord of Yoga.'[191]

An expert in religious movements, the late Dr. John Weldon[192] wrote, "The physical practice of yoga is designed to alter one's consciousness and bring occult transformation. Thus, authoritative texts on both yoga and the occult reveal that yoga is a potentially profound occult practice.[193]

"Yoga," Weldon continued, "is designed to awaken occult energies in the body, to lead to occult transformation, and to secure specific occult goals."

PEOPLE IN DECEPTION TYPICALLY CREATE SUBTER-FUGES

I worked for 25 years as an executive leader in my denomination. Not 50 percent of the time but 100 percent of the time I was involved in disciplinary cases, a deceived individual would create a subterfuge, whether it was a contrived distraction from their sin, or a stratagem to break the focus on their own personal responsibility for the trouble they created by their own sinfulness. Deflecting from their own aberrant actions, they would point out others' lapses or ask unrelated questions about someone else's behaviors or beliefs.

A subterfuge is "an artifice or expedient used to evade a rule, escape a consequence, hide something, etc." Synonyms for subterfuge are: deception, scheme, trick, dodge, or ruse.[194]

When you warn a deceived person of a dangerous practice in which they are involved, he or she will almost always attempt to create a subterfuge. This is an indicator that a deception is actually present. A subterfuge is a scheme, ploy, or contrived scenario designed to deflect the emphasis to something else, with the hopes of cloaking one's own sin or escaping the consequences of their failure.

For example, a few times over the years we dealt with members who had engaged in some kind of adulterous actions. When a deception was present, without genuine repentance, he would say something like, "Well, you don't know my wife and how sneaky she is. I found several phone numbers on the caller ID that I didn't recognize and believe she's been with several different men." Or, "It's just like the church to shoot its wounded. Here I am hurting and vulnerable, and you want to punish me when it was only one time I slipped. You should have known I was going through a tough time, but nobody bothered to call me."

In both cases the deceived man launched a subterfuge of blame. In the first example, he blamed his wife and pointed out her possible failures, trying to make his sin seem not quite so bad. The second example points out how blame shifting creates a distraction from the real issue. It's like when a person gets a speeding ticket for driving 15 miles per hour over the speed limit and instead of admitting his guilt, he blames the police officer for stopping him.

Psalm 141:9 (MSG)
Protect me from their evil scheming, from all their demonic subterfuge.

When a subterfuge is employed, confusion quickly arrives on the scene, and you wonder, "What just happened?" The deceived person attempts to divert your focus to another topic, which they believe will take the spotlight off their deception and put scrutiny on another topic or issue. Instead of seriously consulting with mature believers, they seek to bring justification to their twisted practices or beliefs by conferring with *unqualified* "theologians," inexperienced believers, or biblically unfit teachers. This is a clear sign that a demonic seduction has probably taken hold.

LET ME GIVE YOU AN EXAMPLE

Sally sees her old church friend Molly at the local Walmart and asks what she's been up to lately. "I haven't seen you in church much recently. Are you okay?" Sally asks.

"Oh," Molly says, "I'm doing awesome and have total peace with myself. I joined a Christian Yoga group and we meditate on Jesus as we do our exercise poses and tune up our chakras. I'm healthier than I've ever been and less stressful, thanks to this new way of worshiping the Lord."

"Molly," answers Sally, "I've been reading that some of the top Christian leaders are warning about Christian Yoga, and discovered that it began as an occult practice, and some investigators have even reported that it began as a sex cult."

"Well, I doubt that because it makes me feel so good about myself when I do it. I'm connecting with Jesus like I never did at the church, and I'm encountering the Holy Spirit during my yoga sessions. Besides, I read an article by someone who said Christmas trees began as a Babylonian practice, but we still have one every year. And the last time I was in church, I saw a rainbow in the children's ministry and I know that rainbows represent the New Age Movement. And you still give out candy on Halloween, don't you? Isn't that an occult practice?"

Do you see the subterfuge? By now, poor Sally's head is spinning so fast, she forgot about the yoga and is now wondering about these other matters brought up by Molly. Sally doesn't even know what to say and even starts questioning herself.

When you find yourself in a situation when a subterfuge has been launched, it's best to say something like this: "Molly, I don't know about those things, but right now our focus is on yoga, not Christmas trees, rainbows, muscle-testing, or Halloween. When I have time, I may look into those other matters. Right now, I'm focused on your soul, Molly, and concerned about your practicing of yoga. I'm concerned about you."

Discernment means "to distinguish, to separate out by diligent search, to examine."

Discernment is always related to wisdom. It is our spiritual life preserver. Discernment is the spiritual capability that helps us to make accurate determinations. Unfortunately, some Christians seem to ignore discernment and plunge right into spiritually fatal attractions like yoga. Discernment is our divine defense against deception.

Doing yoga is willful idolatry and is connected to sorcery. [195]

You'll probably find the following five fatal mistakes in almost every professing Christian who joins a yoga class, or follows any other New Age spiritual deception for that matter.

Christians who stray into a deception commonly:

1. Did not seek mature spiritual counsel (Proverbs 1:5; 13:20)

2. Did not seek the counsel of the Lord (Joshua 9:14; Acts 17:11)

3. Did not research the history of the doctrine,

group, or practices in which they are becoming involved (2 Timothy 1:7; 2 Timothy 2:15)

4. Did not investigate the credentials, backgrounds, certifications, and licensing of their teachers (1 Thessalonians 5:21–22; 1 John 4:1)

5. Did not exercise discernment, which is available to all believers (Hebrews 5:14)

> **1 Timothy 4:1-2 (NLT)**
> [1] Now the Holy Spirit tells us clearly that in the last times some will turn away from the true faith; they will follow deceptive spirits and teachings that come from demons.
>
> [2] These people are hypocrites and liars, and their consciences are dead.

Deception can lead to serious dangers.

15

A DANGEROUS FORM OF EXERCISE?

A Useless Way to Get Fit

*For bodily exercise profits a little, but godliness
is profitable in all things, holding promise for the
present life and also for the life to come.*
~ 1 Timothy 4:8 MEV

This modern world is rapidly being prepared for the appearance of the supreme deception of this age—the Antichrist. Every little deception, as I have already warned, can lead to a major grand delusion. (2 Thessalonians 2:9-10)

Deception is always an undercover strategy. A person drifting into deception doesn't fully recognize the lure. The victim does not realize he's been a target. Like a good bear trap, deception is hidden until the victim is ensnared, to be realized only after it's too late.

Often a Christian will sense something amiss before stepping into the trap. That is the Holy Spirit's advance warning system. If he listens and responds, he is delivered. However, if he ignores the discernment, he'll begin to assure his concerned friends and loved ones that everything's all right. Like a drug addict or an alcoholic, he'll deny the lure of the deception that's pulling him into an "off-limits" and dangerous area.

One yoga instructor confessed that *the purpose of yoga classes is to indoctrinate the student with Hindu philosophy.*[196]

The Religion and American Law Blog (Bucknell University) discussed cases of yoga being introduced to children in schools, and parents' reactions to it.

> They wrote, "In American culture today, one might laugh at the idea that yoga is a religious practice. Yoga classes are taught in most gyms and there are studios all over the country, teaching a variety of forms of yoga...The Hindu American Foundation even claims that yoga and Hindu philosophy cannot be separated and that yoga is 'a Hindu way of life.' Religious practice aside, few deny that there is a spiritual component to yoga, the word itself meaning basically 'to unite' or 'to join together,' and this component is definitely entwined with philosophical and theological thought of Asian religious traditions."[197]

Jeremiah 17:2-3 (NLT)
[2] Even their children go to worship at their pagan
altars and Asherah poles,
beneath every green tree and on every high hill.
[3] So I will hand over my holy mountain— along
with all your wealth and treasures and your pagan
shrines—as plunder to your enemies, for sin runs
rampant in your land.

The late Caryl Matrisciana, born and raised in India, was once an avid New Age practitioner of yoga. She said it all in one simple phrase: "Yoga, a practice synonymous with Hindu philosophy. There is no separating yoga from Hinduism." [198]

IT TURNS OUT YOGA IS NOT SUCH A GREAT EXERCISE AFTER ALL

You've probably heard that yoga is good exercise. Maybe even a doctor or some authority told you that yoga is a healthy practice. Maybe some yoga marketer tried to sell you on the benefits of yoga. They certainly promise you a lot:

Through yoga, they claim you can:

1. Increase your flexibility

2. Increase muscle tone and strength

3. Improve your circulatory health

4. Improve your cardio health

5. Sleep better

6. Increase your energy levels

7. Improve athletic performance

8. Reduce injuries

9. Detoxify your organs

10. Improve your posture

11. Help overcome anxiety and depression

12. Help relieve chronic pain

13. Release endorphins that improve your mood

14. ...And so much more

Yes, the yoga marketers promise you much, but it turns out they deliver little.

The facts suggest that yoga is hardly a good form of exercise and stretching.

"According to a study by the American Council on Exercise, a national nonprofit organization that certifies fitness instructors and promotes physical fitness, dedicated yoga practitioners show **no improvements in cardiovascular health.**"

"**It's not the best way to lose weight either.** A typical 50-min. class of Hatha Yoga, one of the most popular styles of yoga in the United States, burns off fewer calories than are in three Oreos—about the same as a slow 50-min. walk." [199]

DID YOUR YOGA INSTRUCTOR CAUTION YOU ABOUT POTENTIAL INJURIES?

"Today orthopedic surgeons, physical therapists and chiropractors across the country are dealing with the increasing fallout from yoga gone awry. **Over the past three years, 13,000 Americans were treated in an emergency room or a doctor's office for yoga-related** injuries, according to the Consumer Product Safety Commission."[200]

Heath Henning of *Truth Watchers* wrote, "We are bombarded with the idea that yoga is not only a healthy exercise for the physical body, but the mind as well. Once again, the statistics show otherwise."[201] 76% of cases experienced psychological disorders.[202]

Not only is yoga basically a useless way to get fit, it is also a dangerous form of exercise.[203]

I would never take my theological doctrines from a cult book, yet they sometimes reveal hidden facts about their beliefs that cannot be overlooked. Ernest Wood who wrote the book *Seven Schools of Yoga*, (originally titled *The Occult Training of the Hindus*) had a few things to say about the potential dangers of yoga.

> "Many people have brought upon themselves incurable illness and even madness by practicing without providing the proper conditions of body and mind."

> "I should like to make it clear that I am not recommending these practices, as I hold that all Hatha Yoga are extremely dangerous…"[204]

The big question I ask: Why haven't most yoga instructors in America given any warnings to students before allowing them to sign up for a yoga class? Look at all the warnings today, just from a physical standpoint (and this is just the tip of the iceberg; a small sampling of the warnings):

Study Finds Yoga Injuries Are on the Rise[205]

"If you've gotten hurt during a yoga class, you're not alone. A new study found that yoga injuries are on the rise ..."

How Yoga Can Wreck Your Body [206] by William J. Broad/New York Times: "... the vast majority of people should give up yoga altogether. It's simply too likely to cause harm." (Quote from a yoga teacher).

Yoga is More Risky for Causing Musculoskeletal Pain than You Might Think.[207] A University of Sydney Report June 27, 2017 says, **Yoga injury rate is up to ten times higher than previously reported.**

In an ABC news piece by Inga Stünzner on April 9, 2018, it reads, **"Yoga injuries land more people in hospital than ever before."**[208]

Yoga Can Be Dangerous: Troubling Recent Finding: For one year, researchers tracked more than 350 people who took yoga classes. Nearly 11 percent of the participants developed a new pain problem, often lasting a few months. And 21percent reported that yoga had aggravated existing injuries.[209]

POSING A RISK? THE STROKE DANGERS OF YOGA POSTURES

Yoga exercises may in fact cause significant harm to your joints, bones and potentially more. Did you know that stroke is one potential consequence of yoga poses even in younger people?

"A Columbia University College of Physicians and Surgeons research team compiled a worldwide survey: The largest number of injuries occurred in the lower back, followed by shoulder, knee and neck. **The next most** common yoga-related consequence: Stroke." [210]

HERE'S A CHECKLIST FOR YOU:

- If you are or have ever been involved in yoga, did you first check the credentials of the teacher?
- Did the teacher immediately express concern about you as a person?
- Did the instructor show an interest in your health and in your health goals?
- Did your yoga instructor ask you about any pre-existing medical conditions?
- Did your yoga instructor ask to check your blood pressure before and after your yoga workout?
- Did your yoga instructor ask you if you suffered from glaucoma or any other eye disease?
- Did your instructor confirm that you were in the proper physical condition to perform yoga postures?
- Did your yoga instructor caution you about the potential physical risks to yoga?
- Did your yoga instructor clearly teach you about the history of yoga or did you hear the same old New Age clichés: "Yoga isn't owned by one religion. Yoga is neutral. It's the intention we set that's important. Yoga helps you to connect with God."

I'm not telling you what to do, but I would run. Those relationships aren't worth sacrificing my true spiritual life...

or my future!

In the next chapter, we'll begin to investigate how an entire nation can be affected demonically by yoga. For now, however, let me close this chapter with two beautiful quotes from two wonderful godly people.

> *"Discernment is a quality of attentiveness to God that, over time, develops into the ability to sense God's heart and purpose in any given moment."*
>
> ~ *Ruth Haley Barton* [211]

> *"Anything that dims my vision for Christ, or takes away my taste for Bible study, or cramps me in my prayer life, or makes Christian work difficult, is wrong for me; and I must, as a Christian turn away from it."*[212]
>
> ~ *J. Wilbur Chapman (1859-1918)*
> *American Pastor and Evangelist*

16

YOGA CRAZE IN HITLER'S THIRD REICH

Summoning Demons Just Before the Rise of the Holocaust

Intelligent people are always ready to learn.
Their ears are open for knowledge.
~ Proverbs 18:15 NLT

The name "Adolf Hitler" stirs emotion in people's hearts still today. Some drudge up feelings of disgust, horror, and contempt. Others not so much.

For example, many people in India are still enamored by Adolf Hitler. Even to this day, Hitler's *Mein Kampf* is still extremely popular. You cannot miss seeing this book lining the shelves of India's top bookstores.[213]

Hitler was fascinated with Hinduism according to Mathias Tieke, author of *Yoga in the Third Reich. Concepts,*

YOGA CRAZE IN THE LAST DAYS

Contrasts, Consequences.[214] It's interesting that Hitler took one of the most prominent symbols of ancient India as his own—the swastika.

HITLER: THE "POSITIVE CHRISTIAN"

Hitler described himself as a "Positive Christian."[215] Positive Christianity was a movement within Nazi Germany which syncretized ideas of racial purity, Hindu philosophies, Nazi ideology, and elements of Christianity.[216]

Germany was a modern, industrialized nation with a large Christian population, so Hitler knew he would have to convince the voters that he too was a Christian, while keeping his Eastern mysticism and Hindu occult practices a secret.

Hitler's "Positive Christianity" was anything but genuine Christianity.

Similarly, the Christian Yoga brands today add a little Christianity to their Hindu philosophies and practices and call it "Christian" or "holy." I'm not suggesting that those involved in Christian Yoga are Nazis, nonetheless, there exists the same type of syncretism in Christian Yoga brands as appeared in Hitler's brand of Christianity.

Positive Christianity may sound really good to some; however, the "Positive Christianity" of the Nazis was not dependent on "faith in Christ as the Son of God" as genuine Christianity teaches.

The self-styled "Positive Christianity" promoted by the Nazi party:

1. Denied the Jewish origins of Christ and the Bible

2. Did not depend on faith in Jesus Christ as the Son of God

3. Incorporated facets of Vedic Hinduism

4. Included antisemitism, racism

5. Advocated the practice of yoga

Hans Kerrl, the Nazi Minister for Church Affairs, claimed that Hitler was the "herald of a new revelation."

What was this new revelation? It was this: "Real Christianity" was not dependent upon the Apostle's Creed or faith in Christ, but on what was determined by the Nazi party.

Kerrl announced, "...And the German people are now called by the party and especially the Fuehrer to a real Christianity."[217]

About the time Hitler coined the term "Positive Christianity" in 1920 as part of the Nazi Party Platform, yoga started becoming a trendy, vogue exercise in Germany.

Hitler's mistress, Eva Braun, enthusiastically practiced yoga.[218] You can still find pictures of her doing yoga poses. Braun and Hitler finally married, but their marriage lasted only forty hours, then they both committed suicide.

HITLER YOGA MATS ON SALE TODAY!

Today you can find "Adolf Hitler Yoga Mats"[219] on sale for those yogis who still honor and adore the murderous maniac. Imagine doing yoga on a mat with Hitler's picture.

Here in America, for the first time ever, the White House established "The Yoga Garden" on the property of the president's residence. When she was the First Lady, Michelle Obama introduced the Yoga Garden at her first Easter Egg Roll in 2009 as part of her "Let's Move! Initiative" and the program grew each year during Obama's presidency.[220]

And now, according to reports, Obama's Presidential Center being built in Chicago will be the first ever to include a "Yoga Room."[221]

The 1920's saw a huge rise in the popularity of yoga in Germany with over fifty yoga books published in Berlin alone. It became a craze among middle-class workers, much the way it is today in America.

The yoga practitioners in Germany—even Christians— had no idea what "gods" or demons they were summoning to their nation through this Hindu ritual.

It seems that a mass delusion like a huge dark blanket descended upon the people of Germany, after which they elected Adolf Hitler as Chancellor in 1933.

A French Hindu writer wrote about her belief that Hitler was an avatar of lord Vishnu, one of the gods of yoga.[222]

After several months of researching the practice of yoga, I learned of something called the *"collective kundalini awakening."*[223] As I understand it, this phenomenon is a peculiar event involving a mass incitement of the "kundalini spirit" in an entire group of people, perhaps an entire nation or tribe, depending on how many people they can get involved in doing yoga poses.

"Awakening the Kundalini" is an expression used by Eastern mystics, yoga gurus, and New Age adherents. They claim a serpent spirit called "kundalini" resides in human beings at the base of the spine, and through yogic body positioning and meditation one can raise the kundalini upward through seven spiritual "chakras" located along the spine. The goal is to heighten this serpent spirit to the "crown chakra" at the top of the skull, bringing about a spiritual-like hypnotic awakening.

The "kundalini spirit" is a term that apologists often use to describe the counterfeit Holy Spirit that shows up through the repeated practice of yoga.

A COLLECTIVE AWAKENING

I wonder if this is what happened in Germany as a result of the extensive national yoga mania; that some demonic critical mass was reached that released an evil, deceiving kundalini spirit over the nation? If so, could this be one of the future Antichrist's inroads to power, bringing the prophesied damning "strong delusion" spoken of by the Apostle Paul in 2 Thessalonians 2:9-12?

In Germany, the yoga rage continued to spread rapidly, much the same as it is in contemporary America. Today we see all kinds of new yoga brands popping up: "Hot Yoga," "Holy Yoga," "Praise Works Yoga," "Jesus Yoga," "God Yoga," "Christian Yoga," "Faith Yoga," and the list goes on. Are they unintentionally calling for a "collective awakening" in America, as Germany experienced just before her darkest hour?

By 1935, the Nazis began arresting pastors who held to the true faith in Jesus Christ. These pastors refused to accept the Nazi government's syncretistic "Positive Christianity" and instead chose to stay true to biblical Christianity. Many like Dietrich Bonhoeffer suffered imprisonment and execution from 1935–1945. Why? The reason: disagreement with the Nazi doctrine and maintaining true faith in Jesus Christ.[224]

Yoga studios continued multiplying throughout the country.

By 1941, the implementation of the "Final Solution" (the plan to execute all European Jews) began. The mass murder of Jewish people, Christians, Gypsies, dissenters, and the handicapped, began as the Nazi regime stormed through Europe setting up and implementing death camps.

Heinrich Himmler, obsessed with the occult, mysticism, and yoga, became the chief architect of "extermination camps," using yoga's ancient Sanskrit texts to justify the Holocaust. He regarded the Sanskrit as a blueprint for cruelty and terror, using it to ultimately justify the mass murders he carried out. One of Himmler's interests was in the Rig Veda, which is imbued with much violence. He identified with the old Indian Kshatriya caste and its attitude of unscrupulous killing for one's 'higher purpose.' [225]

Himmler always carried an ancient text on yoga wherever he went. Eventually, he gleefully enjoyed the "extermination" of an estimated 14 million people including Jews, Christians, Gypsies, non-Aryans, and non-compliers.[226]

How could a normal human being watch, or participate

in, the mass torture and brutal wholesale slaughter of innocent men, women, boys and girls? How is it possible that anyone with a conscience could involve themselves in the unspeakable acts of cruelty unleashed on the Jewish people, Gypsies, and other innocent people, and still remain sane?[227]

What did Himmler's SS[228] recommend as a solution to ease the soldiers', executioners', and guards' consciences? **Yoga!** The SS in Nazi Germany prescribed its members—including death camp guards—to practice yoga, promising that it would enrich their 'minds, bodies, and spirits.'[229]

This leaves us with a nagging question: Are those who practice yoga actually cauterizing their consciences and becoming hard-hearted toward the truth?

1 Timothy 1:19 (NLT)
Cling to your faith in Christ, and keep your conscience clear. For some people have deliberately violated their consciences; as a result, their faith has been shipwrecked.

If yoga is really not that great of an exercise, is saturated with Hinduism, and carries the potential of attracting foreign gods (demons), then what is it about yoga that attracts certain people?

What is it about falsely-called Christian Yoga that attracts certain types of individuals? What's the uncanny and peculiar appeal?

17

WHAT IS THE WEIRD, ABNORMAL APPEAL?

What Magnetizes Some To Yoga?

*For we do not wrestle against flesh and blood,
but against the rulers, against the authorities,
against the cosmic powers over this present darkness, against the spiritual forces of evil in the
heavenly places.*
~ *Ephesians 6:12 (ESV)*

Why do some become magnetized and obsessed by this
Hindu ritual of yoga when other exercises are proven to
be better and more effective? There are hundreds of more
scientific, medically safe exercises not connected to any
form of Eastern mysticism. Even *Consumer Reports Magazine*
warned about the hidden dangers of yoga, including stroke,
joint and muscle damage, and infections.[230]
What is yoga's unearthly allurement? Why not Pilates or

a hundred other better modern exercises? Why does yoga wield such a powerful captivation? What's the pull; the hook?

Is it possible that the same serpent spirit that attracted Eve to that which was off limits is attracting millions into yoga today with the demonic hopes of bringing a "collective deception" in preparation for the end-time delusion? It happened in Germany, and it could happen in your country.

Yoga is not only a pagan practice, it's a culture that drags you down to its level of immaturity. God, on the other hand, brings the best out of you and develops a well-formed maturity in you.[231] Satan, the thief, wishes to stop or block true spiritual maturity. So, he entices the immature believer into forbidden practices.

Correspondent Elspeth Reeve writes in *The Atlantic*, "Yoga is the greatest fraud ever perpetuated against American women...Yoga is fake exercise."[232]

If that is true, what's the enchantment toward yoga? Could it be that the gods of yoga (demons) *really are* setting a lure to snag and hook another victim?

Someone may say, *"I practice yoga and nothing bad has happened to me."* Well, let me tell you a true story.

I was 20 years old, in the U.S. Navy attached to the USS Buck. Our ship was going into dry dock for about six months, so I, along with three of my Navy buddies, rented a house in San Diego for six months. One evening I decided to make some hot turkey sandwiches for the guys and me. I found a thirty-two ounce can of turkey, so carelessly I put the can on the stove and turned the fire on. I figured I'd heat it up that way and not dirty a pan that I'd have to wash later. But I made one little mistake. I failed to open the can. (Did I hear someone say "stupid"?)

I placed the canned turkey on low heat and went to the living room to read while I was waiting. Everything seemed fine. Nothing bad happened. Then after a while, BOOM! It sounded like a bomb went off in the kitchen. We all ran to see what happened and found turkey all over the walls, the ceiling, and the floor—everywhere. What a mess. Now I wasn't thinking about washing a little pan, but the tedious, exhausting task of cleaning up the entire kitchen. What a job.

Miscalculations can be costly.

I was 20 years old and didn't realize you're supposed to open the can to heat it up. The pressure built up in the can until it reached a detonation point, and exploded!

That's exactly how it is with sin and involvement in worship practices not prescribed by the real Master, God. You begin, and at first everything seems fine. You look forward to the "benefits" the way I looked forward to a hot turkey sandwich. However, if something is missing or not right, eventually it blows up. Then it's too late.

You may begin yoga with the best of intentions. You may start slow, on "low heat." Sooner or later there comes an explosion in your life because you didn't realize the real personal threat of your practice, just as I didn't realize the peril of putting a sealed can on the stove.

For me, thankfully, nobody was in the kitchen at the time of the explosion. What if the flying can had become a missile and hit someone in the head? And what if the credible, godly Christian leaders are right in what they're saying about the *spiritual* hazards of yoga? Who will suffer? Someone you love?

WHAT IS YOGA'S MYSTERIOUS ATTRACTION?

Deep down inside, we all long for fulfilling relationships and an escape from the humdrum of our daily lives. We all want to reach beyond ourselves towards a greater "Being." We long for more peace, tranquility, and wholeness. God's Word, the Bible, addresses all these issues and not once is yoga mentioned as a solution.

Think about it. All these yoga teachers keep telling us that yoga was created thousands of years ago and that yoga predates Hinduism. However, ancient people didn't understand the cardiovascular system, blood vessel system, nervous system, glandular system, and how the human physical systems are interrelated.

If yoga is not a good exercise system, what's the attraction to it? People who want to practice yoga are not only attracted to the promises of physical improvement but are lured by the spiritual implications—and snap—they're seduced into an idolatrous religion without even realizing it or believing it's even possible.

Here's a good question. Would you rather drive an old, rusty, worn-out, undependable car or would you prefer a newer, more advanced automobile? Most of us would choose a newer car. So why do people choose an old, ancient practice that is barely satisfactory just from a physical standpoint? From a spiritual perspective, how has yoga worked anything good in India?

Today there are thousands of educated, trained fitness experts that understand the body's systems and how they interrelate. They have studied anatomy, muscles, arteries, heart, and brain and can plan an exercise program that is tailored just for you, and one that is best for you based on your current health condition.

The other option is you can swagger off to a preppy "yoga trainer" who offers nothing but ancient postures.

W. R. Russell, F.R.C.P. published his research on "Yoga and the Vertebral Arteries" in the *British Medical Journal.* He wrote, "If we are to believe that yoga exercises were developed centuries before the circulation of the blood was discovered, it may be wise to point out that the extreme degrees of neck flexion and extension and rotation during some of these exercises (for example, "shoulder stand" or "cobra") must, for some people, be hazardous to the vertebral and anterior spinal artery circulation."[233]

Could the magnetic appeal of yoga be demonic? Those who have been delivered from yoga through faith in the real Jesus Christ testify this is true.[234]

You may be interested in looking up the writings of Beth Eckert, a former New Ager and yoga practitioner, who speaks extensively about the deceptions of yoga, especially so-called "Christian Yoga" on the webpage *"The Other Side of Darkness."*[235]

CAPTIVATED BY A LIE

During the prophesied tribulation period,[236] people all over the world will be captivated by a man with an enormously magnetic personality. They will adore him.

St. John sees into the spirit realm and reveals that they are actually worshipping the dragon/serpent (Satan) but they don't seem to know it. They apparently have no idea that Satan is energizing the "beast"—the final world leader before Jesus returns to Earth.

Revelation 12:9 (NKJV)
So the great dragon was cast out, that serpent of old, called the Devil and Satan, who deceives the whole world; he was cast to the earth, and his angels were cast out with him.

"You may claim to love Jesus but your life proves you are still walking in darkness—confused, befuddled and foggy! When you are truly in love with Jesus, conversing with Him, He turns up the light. There is no darkness at all in His presence. The worst possible darkness to mankind is not in the hearts of God-hating Communist leaders or Christ-hating atheists. It is, rather, the horrible darkness that blinds so-called Christians who refuse to walk in the light."   *~David Wilkerson*

Satan will use his own spiritual power to grant the coming Antichrist a powerful preternatural appeal.[237] Through this deceptive world leader, Satan will charm the world and cast a spell over people. People will be strangely drawn to this spellbinding leader because Satan himself will give him *"a mouth speaking great things."*[238]

It won't be the man's natural power, attractiveness, or oratory skills that will bewitch the people of Earth during that Tribulation time. It will actually be Satan's power working in the Antichrist that will enchant the world.

Billions will be swooning and going crazy with their unnatural admiration for this satanically possessed man. There will be a hypnotic-like mist descending upon the world's population. This satanic darkness will penetrate the population exactly like it did in Hitler's Germany, only more so. Most will view it as "positive;" just the way most in Germany viewed "Positive Christianity." Hitler's reign was but a mere preview of what is approaching now.

> "All of the Eastern religions of today are ultimately traceable to ancient Babylon, where the post-Flood rebellion against God began."
>
> ~ Gary Kah[239]

Hindu practices, like yoga, along with the Hindu myths that go with it, actually originated in ancient Babylon, where all false religious practices began. The Babylonian spirit will once again experience a resurgence, captivating the world in the last days according to John the Revelator.

Revelation 17:5 (NKJV)
And on her forehead a name was written:
MYSTERY, BABYLON THE GREAT, THE
MOTHER OF HARLOTS AND OF THE
ABOMINATIONS OF THE EARTH.

Respected English archeologist and historian Alexander Hislop, author of *The Two Babylons*, traced Babylon's Mystery Religion, first to Egypt and then to India. He identified Isa as the counterfeit Jesus of Hinduism and revealed that *"Hindu mythology is admitted to be essentially Babylonian."*[240]

Babylon is the mother of all mystery religions including:[241]

1. All Eastern mysticism
2. Hinduism
3. Theosophy
4. Free Masonry
5. Yoga
6. Occult 'sciences'
7. New Age
8. And many other metaphysical-type cultic groups

Yoga instructors (whether they realize it or not), could be opening up their students to actual demonization, or possibly an active type of oppression. This may be done naïvely or deliberately in some cases.

Here's the question: Do demons care if a person is innocent and has good motives or intentions? No! A demon's role is to destroy. A demon is not a little pet you can train to do tricks. A demon comes to do the work of his master, Satan, to steal, kill, and destroy.

John 10:10 (NKJV)
The thief does not come except to steal, and to kill, and to destroy. I have come that they may have life, and that they may have *it* more abundantly.

It's outright bizarre when you hear "Holy Yoga" teachers say yoga becomes holy if your intention is right. That's like saying, "I can check my horoscope because I intend to find God's will that way."

I suppose I could re-intention my car to be a washing machine. It's no longer a Buick because my intention is that it be a washing machine. Regardless of my intention, I can throw my dirty clothes in the car...and I still end up with a pile of dirty clothes. Likewise, I could see a beehive and re-intention it to be a friendly cat. But when I pet the "cat," I get stung...really bad!

Galatians 1:6-9 (ESV)
I am astonished that you are so quickly deserting him who called you in the grace of Christ and are turning to a different gospel— not that there is another one, but there are some who trouble you and want to distort the gospel of Christ. But even if we or an angel from heaven should preach to you a gospel contrary to the one we preached to you, let him be accursed. As we have said before, so now I say again: If anyone is preaching to you a gospel contrary to the one you received, let him be accursed.

YOGA: A PROGRESSIVE PATHWAY TO THE OCCULT

Once students begin on the path of yoga—any kind of yoga—they almost always find themselves curiously being pulled into deeper areas of occult spirituality. In other words, the reason why certain people began yoga is not the reason they continue. Something like a hook snags them to go deeper.

Psychology Today published an article on why people get involved in yoga. They found that 90 percent of those who begin yoga classes come looking for "greater flexibility, stress relief, health, and physical fitness. But for most of them, after a while, *their primary reason changed to spiritual reasons* or the hope of reaching "self-actualization" and "self-awareness."[242]

Even Swamie Mukerji agrees that the real motivation of yoga is the development of spiritual consciousness. He wrote, "The Spiritual Consciousness...is the motive prompting to the practice of Yoga."[243]

The question is which side of the spirit realm does the practice of yoga attract?

Yoga is a form of occult-like worship in Hinduism. Many of the asana poses honor Hindu deities. The system of yoga is designed to create a desire for the participant to move into deeper states in preparation for advancing the person to even deeper forms of Hinduism. Little by little, the yoga spirits take you deeper into occult darkness and oppression.

And...the gods of yoga are shockingly gruesome and frightful.

18

CHAPTER

THE TERRIFYING
GODS OF YOGA

The Triumvirate of Demon Gods

*Take heed to yourselves that your heart be not
deceived, and you turn away and serve other gods
and worship them.*
~ *Deuteronomy 11:16 MEV*

In yoga, there exists the belief that a triumvirate of
demon gods, Brahma, Vishnu, and Shiva are the spiritual
magistrates jointly ruling over those who practice yoga. A
triumvirate is defined as a coalition of three magistrates or
rulers for joint administration.[244]

A triumvirate is not to be confused with the word
"trinity." Christians believe in a triune God, eternally
existent in three distinct persons (Father, Son, and Holy
Spirit), yet One. "The Lord our God is one God."[245] The

yogic Hindus are polytheists (many gods) and some sects, pantheistic (God is in everything).

REDUCING JESUS CHRIST TO A GURU

Like the occult and New Age, Hinduism embraces many religious ideas as opposed to a single, organized religion. Hinduism has no one founder but is instead a fusion or syncretizing of various beliefs, exactly like the Christian Yoga brands have done.

Jesus is often reduced to a mere guru.[246]

Yoga shirts sport the words, "Jesus is my guru," *not*, "Jesus is my Lord."

Hare Krishna's claim was "Jesus is my Guru."[247] "Concerning Jesus Christ, a writer for the Hare Krishna Temple teaches, 'He [Jesus] is our guru. He is preaching God consciousness, so he is our spiritual master.'"[248]

How can some professing Christians get involved in a Hindu practice like yoga? In his article, "Spiritual Counterfeits," The late Evangelist David Wilkerson gave his answer, "A great majority of church-going believers have never been saved!"[249] It's true; people by nature love darkness more than light (John 3:19).

In Hinduism, we find one supreme demon-god, Brahman. Though there are millions of other gods and goddesses, many Hindus believe they are each an expression of the main god, Brahman. Other Hindus believe that Brahman is merely a person's "higher self" that can be actualized through yoga, breathing techniques, and "mindfulness" (Eastern meditation). Either way, or in any of its other various combinations, all Hinduism runs counter to credible biblical teaching.

That's probably why the yoga teachers like the late Paramahansa Yogananda found it necessary to reinterpret the Bible from a Hindu viewpoint. One of Yogananda's chief aims was to "reveal the complete harmony and basic oneness of original Christianity as taught by Jesus Christ and original yoga as taught by Bhagavan Krishna, and to show that these principles of truth are the common scientific foundation of all true religions."[250]

Yogananda's syncretistic blending of Christianity with Hindu philosophy and practice sounds eerily familiar today among the "Christian Yoga" advocates. In the United States, Yogananda, a Hindu, was actually the founder of "Christian Yoga."

When you read Yogananda's writings, you'll notice biblical Scriptures are given a strange "twist." Those who have neglected to build a strong understanding of God's Word, God's character and God's nature become easy targets for this syncretistic religious teaching.

Yogananda was a mannerly man, I understand, to be admired for his gentleness, kindness, and alleged generosity. However, his teachings may be exactly what the prophets warned about when they said:

1 Timothy 4:1 (NKJV)
"Now the Spirit expressly says that in latter times some will depart from the faith, giving heed to deceiving spirits and doctrines of demons"

2 Timothy 4:3-4 (NKJV)
"For the time will come when they will not
endure sound doctrine; but after their own lusts
shall they heap to themselves teachers, having
itching ears; And they shall turn away their ears
from the truth, and shall be turned unto fables."

Other yoga instructors followed his lead by subtly claiming the Bible cannot be trusted, unless you accept the yoga teacher's interpretations and twists. The Scripture twisting even in "Christian Yoga" brands is disgraceful.

Here's just one of the twisted explanations of God's Word that abounds in yoga teachings, although the Christian brands twist more subtly.

Concerning Jesus' claim of being the Way, the Truth and the Life, one author, writing about "the Christ Consciousness" said, *"The 'me' Jesus referred to isn't himself, but rather the Self within you. You don't find God through Jesus, you find God within yourself."* [251]

Let us take a look at what God says about twisting His Truth:

Isaiah 24:5 (NLT)
The earth suffers for the sins of its people, for
they have twisted God's instructions, violated his
laws, and broken his everlasting covenant.

A promoter of "Jesus Yoga" said, *"Yoga means the way and Jesus is the way, the truth, and the life and Jesus brings you to God. Jesus Yoga has 12 steps that will lead you to salvation, enlightenment, the purpose of your life, the Christ Consciousness, and the new Pentecost."* [252]

Excuse me, but yoga does not mean "the way." It means "yoke" or "union" typically with yogic gods or one's "higher self."

Twelve steps leading to salvation? This is a real twist from the truth, and I feel badly for young Christians who get involved in this type of Jesus Yoga. Here is the truth:

Acts 15:11 (NLT)
We believe that we are all saved the same way, by the undeserved grace of the Lord Jesus."

Ephesians 2:5 (NLT)
that even though we were dead because of our sins, he gave us life when he raised Christ from the dead. (It is only by God's grace that you have been saved!)

Ephesians 2:8 (NLT)
God saved you by his grace when you believed. And you can't take credit for this; it is a gift from God.

2 Timothy 1:9 (NLT)
For God saved us and called us to live a holy life. He did this, not because we deserved it, but because that was his plan from before the beginning of time—to show us his grace through Christ Jesus.

To many yogis, reaching the Christ Consciousness through yoga is how they define being "born again." Sometimes they rename the kundalini awakening as "The New Pentecost." The kundalini spirit of yoga mimics the Holy Spirit.

I saw one Christian brand of yoga advertising, *"Hidden and ancient techniques of Christian meditation."* Remember, "hidden" means "occult." It's a dead give-away.

YOGA'S DEMON GODS:

Brahma

Brahma is known as a creator god in Hinduism, not to be confused with Brahman who is worshiped by Hindus as the supreme God force present within all things. Brahma has four faces, one in each direction. Brahma is also known as "Svayambhu" (meaning self-born), and "Vāgīśa" (lord of speech), and the creator of the four Vedas (ancient Hindu scriptures), one from each of his four mouths.[253]

Brahma had several wives.[254] He is the least worshiped of the three yogic demon-gods for a very good reason.

The Hindu story goes like this: Brahma created a daughter, Shatarupa, to assist him in his task of creation. She was so beautiful that Brahma became infatuated with her, and lusted after her wherever she went, thus embarrassing her. In every direction Shatarupa went, Brahma sprouted a new head until he had four, one in each direction. When Shatarupa tried to get away from Brahma's lustful looks, she jumped up into the air, and Brahma sprouted a fifth head on top of all the rest.[255]

Shiva came along and rebuked Brahma for demonstrating lustful and incestuous thoughts and chopped off his fifth head for unholy behavior. Since Brahma had distracted his mind towards the craving of the flesh, Shiva put a curse on him that people should not worship him.

Vishnu

Vishnu is the second god in the Hindu yogic triumvirate. Hindus believe that he has been reincarnated nine times so far (once as Krishna), and will be reincarnated one more time close to the end of this Age.[256]

His hands always carry four objects in them which represent the things for which he is responsible:

1. The 'Om' (or Aum) sound used in yoga representing the primeval sound of creation

2. The chakras (taught in yoga classes)

3. The lotus flower representing a glorious existence and liberation

4. The mace representing mental and physical strength

Vishnu is the demon-god who is supposedly the preserver of the universe, however, in some of his reincarnations, he was not so benevolent.[257]

One of his reincarnations was that of "Parashurama" (Rama with the Ax) and another was "Krishna;" both of whom brought about the deaths of many innocent people.

Shiva

Shiva, a demon-god of Yoga, is also known as "Yogeshwara," lord of yogis (yoga practitioners). He's usually mild-mannered, but whenever he gets angry he opens his third eye and wrecks havoc and releases destruction and ruin. He is a demon-god who is feared. He howls and shoots arrows that spread disease. Shiva's role is to destroy in order to re-create.

Mark Cartwright of the Ancient History Encyclopedia writes about Shiva, "A complex character, he may represent goodness, benevolence and serve as the Protector, but he also has a darker side as the leader of evil spirits, ghosts and vampires and as the master of thieves, villains and beggars." [258]

This yoga deity represents death and dissolution. Shiva is known by many names - Mahadeva, Pashupati, Nataraja, Vishwanath, Bhole Nath, and Yogeshwara (Lord of Yogis).

Shiva instructed worship of his phallus as the symbolic "Linga." The story of how this phallus worship in Hinduism began is too vulgar to summarize in this writing, yet it seems par for course that something sexual would be involved with the "god of yoga."[259]

Accordingly, Shiva is represented as a phallic symbol called the 'Shiva Lingam' or "Shivalinga" in most temples. Many vulgar and obscene stories exist about how the "Lord of Yoga," Shiva, came to be symbolized by a phallus, but if you saw his stature, you'd have a good idea as to why. According to Tantric scholars, the Shiva Lingam represents Shiva's phallus in spiritual form. In some temples sex rituals and perversions of all kinds are considered as offerings to the demon-gods of yoga and Hinduism.

Shivalinga poles are often found in Hindu yoga worship. These are large poles, usually wooden that are shaped like Shiva's "lingam."

In other countries they were known as Asherah poles. This practice gained popularity in Israel whenever God's people thought they could combine God's instructions with pagan practices. This, it seems, is precisely what all the "faithy" brands of yoga have sought to do - mix the unmixable and unintentionally generate deception and confusion.

An Asherah pole was a so-called "sacred pole" used in the worship of the pagan goddess Asherah and sometimes sported an image of her consort, Baal, carved into the pole. The Asherah pole was often mentioned in the Old Testament as one of the ways the Israelites sinned against the Lord and worshiped other gods, which St. Paul told us in the Christian Scriptures were actually demons.[260] They assumedly had no idea they were involved in demonic idolatry.

Worship around the Asherah poles included sexual immorality, divination, and fortune-telling. Moses spoke specifically against Asherah worship (Deuteronomy 16:21). These Asherah poles were exactly like Hindu Shivalinga poles, leading scholars to speculate that this practice was imported from the East, just as Isaiah the prophet said.

Isaiah 2:6 NLT
For the Lord has rejected his people, the descendants of Jacob, because they have filled their land with practices from the East and with sorcerers, as the Philistines do. They have made alliances with pagans.

In essence, an Asherah pole is carved like a giant phallus, just as the Shivalinga of yogic Hinduism. Queen Jezebel worshiped Asherah and supported 400 Asherah prophets (1 Kings 18:19). The sexual relationships and perversity among the false gods set an example for unbridled sensuality among their worshipers.[261]

By looking at the way Israel strayed into the worship of pagan demon-gods, we can see clear parallels confirming that many of the Eastern practices adopted by God's people were identical to Hindu and yogic practices today.

THE YOGA CAKE: WILL YOU EAT IT?

If you were offered a piece of cake that was baked in a clean kitchen facility, you would probably enjoy eating a piece. But suppose there was another kitchen that baked a cake with ten percent dog feces added to the batter. They carefully blended it throughout the batter and baked it perfectly, and added beautiful icing and decorations to the cake. Now, if you knew what was added to the cake mix, would you eat even one crumb of it? Yet people risk their spiritual lives by biting into a "yoga cake" that has disgusting and potentially dangerous ingredients added.

Don't be beguiled by the beauty of the "yoga cake." Pay attention to all the ingredients. Satan will always present his lies as the truth, make them appealing, and promise you benefits for biting into the forbidden fruit.

God forbade these foreign religious practices, like yoga, because He loves you and wants to protect you from the dangers that lie ahead in your life if you participate in them. Israel's and Judah's godly kings always gave their best efforts to stop the people from false worship.

> **2 Kings 23:6 (MSG)**
> He took the obscene phallic Asherah pole from The Temple of God to the Valley of Kidron outside Jerusalem, burned it up, then ground up the

ashes and scattered them in the cemetery.

2 Kings 17:16-17 (MSG)
They threw out everything God, their God, had
told them, and replaced him with two statue-gods
shaped like bull-calves and then a phallic pole
for the whore goddess Asherah. They worshiped
cosmic forces—sky gods and goddesses—and
frequented the sex-and-religion shrines of Baal.

2 Kings 23:13-14 (MSG)
The king proceeded to make a clean sweep of all
the sex-and-religion shrines that had proliferated
east of Jerusalem on the south slope of Abomination Hill, the ones Solomon king of Israel
had built to the obscene Sidonian sex goddess
Ashtoreth, to Chemosh the dirty-old-god of
the Moabites, and to Milcom the depraved god
of the Ammonites. He tore apart the altars,
chopped down the phallic Asherah-poles, and
scattered old bones over the sites.

1 Kings 15:11-13 (MSG)
Asa conducted himself well before God, reviv-
ing the ways of his ancestor David. He cleaned
house: He got rid of the sacred prostitutes and
threw out all the idols his predecessors had made.
Asa spared nothing and no one; he went so far
as to remove Queen Maacah from her position
because she had built a shockingly obscene me-
morial to the whore goddess Asherah. Asa tore it
down and burned it up in the Kidron Valley.

One more interesting fact: Shiva enjoys a consort,
named Kali. She is the dark demon-goddess of destruction.
She is also considered as the goddess of death. Kali, in

most images, is clothed in animal skin with a necklace of skulls hanging from her neck. Kali is perhaps the fiercest among all the Hindu deities. Her tongue protrudes from her mouth, her eyes are red, and her face is smudged with blood. She stands with one foot on the thigh, and another on the chest of her consort, Shiva (the lord of yoga).

Tertullian, an honored and credible Church father (c.155–c.240 AD), also warned Christians about the Hindu and Hindu-like doctrines. Apparently, just as happened in the Old Testament days, there were professing God-followers in the second and third centuries blending elements of polytheism and pantheism into their Christian practice. He preached, "We are not Indian Brahmins or Gymnosophists."[262] Brahmins were Hindu priests and teachers; Gymnosophists were apparently members of a sect of Hindus sometimes known as the "naked monks."

The demon-gods of yoga are ferocious and clearly Hindu. To yogic people, their god (Brahman) coexisted with many gods, goddesses, and spirits.

YOUR ENTIRE FAMILY IS AFFECTED

Deuteronomy 5:9 (NLT)
You must not bow down to them or worship them, for I, the Lord your God, am a jealous God who will not tolerate your affection for any other gods. I lay the sins of the parents upon their children; the entire family is affected—even children in the third and fourth generations of those who reject me.

I pray for those dear Christians who have ill-advisedly,

and perhaps impetuously, hooked up with some kind of yoga purporting to be "Christian" or "holy." I don't ever want to shame a person who mistakenly got involved in such a spiritual hoax. Like St. Paul said to the Corinthians, "This is not to shame you but to warn you."[263]

In the next chapter we want to take a closer look at these Jesus-brand yoga teachers and how they are marketing their businesses to immature and unseasoned Christians.

19

CHAPTER

THE TEACHERS OF YOGA

Are They Hindu Missionaries in Disguise?

*Let no one deceive you with empty words, for
because of these things the wrath of God
is coming ...
~ Ephesians 5:6 MEV*

Yoga has played one of the most influential and key roles
in drawing people into the snare of pagan Eastern religious
thought. Since it is often *presented* as simply exercise, it is
easy to be deceived by it.

The practice of Yoga has existed for thousands of years in
some form or another. It has always been present in pagan
religions, occultism, and mysticism.

Today, many pastors are crying out for the glory of
God to fill their churches and wonder why the spiritual
atmosphere of Heaven seems stifled or blocked. Could it
be that pagan gods (demons) are being summoned secretly

by a few key people in the background who are involved in pagan, "New Age" teaching and idolatrous practices? Small idolatries will spread, hindering and darkening the pastor's vision of revival and the glory of God...if he allows it to continue.

Galatians 5:9 (AMP)
A little leaven [a slight inclination to error, or a few false teachers] leavens the whole batch [it perverts the concept of faith and misleads the church].

This is precisely the reason good pastors and leaders will ferret out the twisted doctrines and practices that pervert faith and mislead church members.

Psalm 101:7-8 (NLT)
[7] I will not allow deceivers to serve in my house, and liars will not stay in my presence.
[8] My daily task will be to ferret out the wicked and free the city of the Lord from their grip.

If you listen carefully to the Christian-brand Yoga teachers, it sounds to me as though they are perverting the Gospel of Jesus Christ, transforming it into something aberrant and freakish. Are they misleading their students into a counterfeit religious practice disguised as exercise?

HOLY YOGA FACED LAWSUIT

Sexual allegations in yoga groups continue to surface. According to the Dallas News, a Texas woman was suing a "Holy Yoga" group, alleging that she was forced out after she complained about an instructor being sexually inappropriate towards her during a class. She claims she was ostracized from "Holy Yoga" after reporting a sexual assault by a fellow female instructor. According to Federal Courts Reporter, Kevin Krause, in the Dallas News, said the lady took legal action against the "Holy Yoga" group.[264]

In the complaint, Article III, 7 - FACTUAL BACKGROUND reads:

"Holy Yoga is a religious organization that touts itself as using yoga to serve as a Christian-focused organization. While Holy Yoga holds itself out as a "ministry," none of the instructors or leaders are required to become ordained ministers, whether they serve as volunteers or full-time employees."[265]

I understand this Galvis vs. Holy Yoga Foundation lawsuit was either settled or terminated in February of 2019. That's good news. You can get the details at Pace Monitor.[266]

Lawsuits are not uncommon in today's litigious society. Not all lawsuits are as they appear to be at first, so I didn't want to speak for or against either side in this case because God's Word teaches us that justice will hear out both sides. Besides Christians are instructed to not sue other Christians (1 Corinthians 6:1-8). Believers are taught to follow a totally different approach to resolving matters with other believers (Matthew 18:15-17).

Proverbs 18:17 (TPT)
There are two sides to every story. The first one to speak sounds true until you hear the other side and they set the record straight.

Nonetheless, yoga seems to have a history of sexual complaints and allegations against its instructors. Not all, but some.

KQED news of San Francisco reported that women globally are opening up and telling their stories of sexual misconduct and abuse in yoga classes.[267]

In the San Francisco news piece, Shannon Roche, chief operating officer of Yoga Alliance admitted, "There is a long history of sexual misconduct and of abuse-of-power situations in the yoga community."

According to the KQED news piece, "Yoga teachers aren't licensed in the U.S. No state agency, such as a medical board, oversees instructors, disciplines or investigates them, or defines their practice."

Yoga teachers are not a gift from God, according to the Bible. Christian teachers, on the other hand, who accurately and skillfully present God's Word *are* a gift from God.[268]

2 Timothy 2:15 (AMP)
Study and do your best to present yourself to God approved, a workman [tested by trial] who has no reason to be ashamed, accurately handling and skillfully teaching the word of truth.

St. Paul was not only an apostle but a teacher, approved by God, unashamed, *accurately and skillfully* teaching the principles of God's Word.

2 Timothy 1:11 (AMP)
...for which I was appointed a preacher and an apostle and a teacher [of this good news regarding salvation].

The prayers of godly Christian teachers are sincere. They cry out, "Show me Your ways, O Lord; Teach me Your paths" (Psalm 25:4 NKJV) and "Lead me in Your truth and teach me, For You are the God of my salvation; On You I wait all the day." (Psalm 25:5 NKJV)

TEACHERS OF LIES

The Holy Spirit speaks frequently of a certain type of teacher—a lying teacher and a false teacher. Habakkuk writes about the "teachers of lies." (Habakkuk 2:18) Jesus Himself warned about these teachers.

> **Matthew 7:15 (AMP)**
> "Beware of the false prophets, [teachers] who come to you dressed as sheep [appearing gentle and innocent], but inwardly are ravenous wolves.

In Acts 20:28-30 the Apostle Paul warned of certain teachers who would speak perversely and distort spiritual matters in an effort to gain followers.

COUNTERFEIT TEACHERS MISLEAD PEOPLE WITH DISTORTIONS OF GOD'S WORD

> **Galatians 1:6-8 (AMP)**
> ⁶ I am astonished *and* extremely irritated that you are so quickly shifting your allegiance and deserting Him who called you by the grace of Christ, for a different [even contrary] gospel;
>
> ⁷ which is really not another [gospel]; but there are [obviously] some [people masquerading as teachers] who are disturbing and confusing you [with a misleading, counterfeit teaching] and want to distort the gospel of Christ [twisting it into something which it absolutely is not].
>
> ⁸ But even if we, or an angel from heaven, should preach to you a gospel contrary to that which we [originally] preached to you, let him be con-

demned to destruction!

ARE UNQUALIFIED TEACHERS INVADING THE CHURCH?

Paul warned his young son in the faith, Timothy, about unqualified and unprofitable teachers that would come into the church and oppose true men and women of God, the way the Egyptian magicians opposed Moses (2 Timothy 3:8).

Practicing just a little false teaching can corrupt your whole being and, worse yet, the whole church!

Paul prophesied of a day when people wouldn't care about accurate instruction based on God's Truth but would choose teachers that support their own error-ridden doctrines.[269]

The Apostle Peter also gave us ample warning about these deceitful, heretical teachers.[270]

John, the beloved apostle, cautioned the Church about deceptive prophets and teachers.[271]

Shameless false teachers will sometimes quote respected and credible leaders, like Francis Chan, Deitrick Bonhoffer, Billy Graham, Greg Laurie, and others, in hopes of inspiring you to believe that they themselves are credible and endorsed by these leaders.

Sadly, church members are sometimes prone to biting into demonic bait and slogans more often than you can imagine. I have grieved over many wandering members over the years that somehow became entangled in weird, twisted theology.

I've seen the pain in their families when everything eventually came crashing down. They chased after a twisted theology; a lie. And pursuing a lie always has the same results. When the destruction comes, fickle followers will weep, saying,

Proverbs 5:13-14 (TPT)
[13] Why didn't I take seriously the warning of my wise counselors? Why was I so stupid to think that I could get away with it?

[14] Now I'm totally disgraced and my life is ruined! I'm paying the price..."

Syncretistic heretics would never have a chance of enjoying a platform in the church if genuine believers would practice good discernment by daily studying what genuine faith looks like.

Half-truths are actually great lies that lead followers down a dangerous path.

The late evangelist David Wilkerson once said, "God hates the lukewarm gospel of half-truths that is now spreading over the Globe. This gospel says, 'Just believe in Jesus and you'll be saved. There's nothing more to it.' It ignores the whole counsel of God, which speaks of repenting from former sins, of taking up your cross, of being conformed to the image of Christ by the refining work of the Holy Spirit. It is totally silent about the reality of hell and an after-death judgment."[272]

HITLER'S PROPAGANDA PRINCIPLES EMPLOYED BY TEACHERS OF FALSE SPIRITUAL IDEOLOGIES

Purveyors of false and crossbred philosophies must rely

on propaganda to promote their aberrant ideas in order to create an **illusion of truth.** This is because the Bible does not support their teaching. A cultist or false teacher is not going to announce, "I'm teaching heresy." In fact, those who are teaching false theologies or practices may not even realize it themselves.

When there is absolutely no biblical, logical, or reasonable foundation for a teaching or practice, twisted teachers will use repetitious propaganda talking points seeking to motivate and lure others into believing and acting on their false teaching. These teachers employ suggestion, repetition, innuendo, simple language, and refuse to admit there is another side.

They often will marginalize anyone who may challenge their beliefs, exactly as they did to the prophets of God who warned of false theology or twisted practices among God's people in the Old and New Testament times.

Jeremiah 8:8-9 (NLT)
8 "'How can you say, "We are wise because we have the word of the LORD," when your teachers have twisted it by writing lies?
9 These wise teachers will fall into the trap of their own foolishness, for they have rejected the word of the LORD. Are they so wise after all?

Next, we'll take a glimpse of the lies that seem like truth to many.

20

THE ILLUSION OF TRUTH

*Repeat a Lie Often Enough
and it Becomes the Truth to Many*
I will not allow deceivers to serve in my
house, and liars will not stay in my presence.
~ Psalm 101:7 NLT

You've probably heard the phrase, *"Repeat a lie often
enough and it becomes the truth."* It actually becomes the
illusion of truth.

Joseph Goebbels, a masterful speaker and propagandist
minister for the German Third Reich under Adolf Hitler,
was responsible for creating a favorable image of the Nazi
party to the German people.[273] He shaped opinions and
attitudes by using just a few talking points and repeating
them over and over again. Goebbels taught that good
propaganda must be limited to a few points continually
repeated.[274] Propaganda must always be simple and
repetitious.[275]

Typically, a false teacher will look and sound so sincere and passionate that, without biblical discernment, you wouldn't know they're actually twisting God's Word. True Christian teachers will "reach for the Bible first, second, and always."[276]

Isaiah 8:20 (NLT)
Look to God's instructions and teachings! People who contradict his word are completely in the dark.

If you hear professing "Christian teachers" trying to blend a contrary or conflictive religious source with Christianity, run for your spiritual life! The only Scriptures Christians regard as God's Word are found in the Holy Bible, Genesis through Revelation. The Bible contains no Sutras, no Sanskrit, and no other books.

TRUE HEROES

Teachers who follow the Lord Jesus Christ admire role models like Paul, Matthew, Mark, Luke, John, Peter, Barnabas, and all the biblical prophets who stood strong for the honor of God. Paramahansa Yogananda, Patañjali, Sadhguru, Judas Iscariot, Absalom, or some swami, guru, or maharishi will *never* be on the true Christian's list of role models or heroes.

THE ILLUSION OF TRUTH

"Repeat a lie often enough and it becomes 'the truth' to many." According to psychologists, this is known as the "illusion of truth" effect.[277] Do you want to make a lie or half-truth seem true? Say it again. And again. And again.

And again.

"Yoga predates Hinduism."

"It is the intention that matters."

"Yoga is spiritual; not religious."

"Same moves; different intention."

"Yoga is God's beautiful gift to the world."

"No religion owns yoga."

"Yoga is not a religion."

"Yoga is nonsectarian."

"Yoga has the ability to deepen your faith."

"Yoga deepens your connection with God."

"Yoga was given to humanity by God."

With cultists and false teachers, the facts don't actually matter. The truth is meaningless to them. Simply repeat a lie over and over again and eventually, you will believe it and so will your followers. This is called "the illusory truth effect." Masters of manipulation understand this principle and employ it successfully.[278]

"If we displease God, does it matter whom we please? If we please Him does it matter whom we displease?" **Leonard Ravenhill,** *Why Revival Tarries: A Classic on Revival*

Jesus said that many would come seeking to deceive or lead astray, even the elect, if possible. Peter encourages us believers to, "gird up the loins of yor mind." (1 Peter 3:13). Satan will use any method possible to lead members of the Body of Christ astray, so he can devour them along with their families (1 Peter 5:8).

The Institute in Basic Life Principles teaches that "A person with the gift of teaching will be **especially alert to and wary of false teachers**. He will want to investigate their backgrounds before listening to them."[279]

WHAT QUALIFIES A "CHRISTIAN YOGA" TEACHER?

That leads us to wonder what qualifications are required for a Christian Yoga teacher. Are those qualifications in writing somewhere? Can a "Christian Yoga" teacher be a member of a false cult? Are there expected doctrinal and morality standards to which the teachers must adhere? How much of the 200 plus hours required of Christian Yoga teachers is about doctrines of the Christian faith and how much is about the yoga sutras and precepts? [225]

Why would any sane person put the safekeeping of their soul in the hands of a teacher who professes Christianity, yet distorts God's Word by adding occult practices to it? You cannot read the entire Bible, believe it, and still conclude that it's not offensive to God to practice what pagan religions practice.

Some American yoga teachers present yoga for what it really is. Their students enter the class with full disclosure of the history, the roots, the religion, and the true purpose, intention, and motivation of yoga. While the teachers may not be Christians, they must be admired for their honesty. They are not deceiving people into yoga by calling it "Holy," "Christian," "Faith," "God," "Praise," "Yahweh," "Pneuma," or "Jesus" Yoga.

The yoga teachers who change the intention of yoga, misapply biblical Scriptures, insert Sanskrit terminology, teach from Patañjali, and present yoga as a holy gift from God without a shred of biblical backing, are either deceived themselves or cleverly disingenuous. Of necessity, they must twist the Word of God to fit their agenda.

> **Jeremiah 8:8-9 (NLT)**
> How can you say, "We are wise because we have the word of the LORD," when your teachers have twisted it by writing lies? These wise teachers will fall into the trap of their own foolishness, for they have rejected the word of the LORD. Are they so wise after all?

Yoga is not and never has been a Christian doctrine or practice.

To assert that "Holy Yoga" or some type of so-called "Christian Yoga" only practices the poses of yoga but not the Hindu worship aspects is preposterous.

Yoga is yoga. It is an ancient practice of posing in various postures before Shiva, Vishnu, and Brahma, the Hindu yogic demon-gods. That's why they are called "poses." You cannot intelligently make a distinction between "Christian Yoga" and "Hindu Yoga." The reason is, as I have already stated, yoga is yoga. Period!

It's completely contrary to reason and common sense to think you can change the nature of yoga by adding a prefix to it or changing its intention. It reveals an utter senselessness in those who accept the concept of re-purposing an ancient pagan practice to one that honors the true and living God.

Golf is golf. There is no regular golf and Christian golf. Think this through sensibly. If I developed a business and called it "Christian golf," and played only three holes because I didn't believe in the other six holes, would it not still be golf? And what if I developed a business plan for "Christian baseball" in which you only had to run to first base and back to home plate because second and third bases are evil, would it not still be baseball? There is no Christian baseball and there is no Christian golf. Baseball is baseball; golf is golf; yoga is yoga. It is what it is.

YOGA STRIPS YOUR SPIRITUAL DEFENSES.

Yoga poses are performances to the Hindu gods. Therefore, when a Christian does yoga, you'll probably notice the performance mentality developing in them. What ministry they once enjoyed, anointed by God, now gradually morphs into merely a performance, whether it's preaching, singing, soul-winning...whatever. Yoga people often tend to become more performance-based rather than anointed and glory-based.

False teachers may mention Jesus here and there, but they will eventually lead you away from His deity, His Gospel, or His power (2 Peter 2:1). Of course, they will not do so openly at first. Even Christian missionaries tell of the difficulty in making disciples for Christ among Hindus. The Hindu followers will hear the Gospel, then accept Jesus as just another of their many gods.

There is absolutely nothing in God's Word anywhere to justify the practice of yoga. In fact, it's just the opposite.

Deuteronomy 12:29-32 (NLT)

[29] "When the LORD your God goes ahead of you and destroys the nations and you drive them out and live in their land,

[30] do not fall into the trap of following their customs and worshiping their gods. Do not inquire about their gods, saying, 'How do these nations worship their gods? I want to follow their example.'

[31] You must not worship the LORD your God the way the other nations worship their gods, for they perform for their gods every detestable act that the Lord hates.

You can try to justify your actions based on your feelings or personal opinions, but remember God is not mocked.[280]

HERE ARE SOME QUESTIONS YOU CAN ASK:

1. Does the "Christian Yoga instructor" teach his or her students about "Chakras"?

If so, it's occult. Each physical posture and stretch was designed specifically for the spiritual awakening of what is referred to in yoga as spinal chakras and in the occult as "energy centers." Did you know that they teach the second chakra stores "sexual energy" and that energy lies dormant until awakened through yoga and controlled breathing?

2. Does the "Christian Yoga instructor" teach his or her students about the "Sutras"?

If so, it's Occultism and Hinduism. Do these following Sutras sound compatible with God's teaching from the Bible?

- Sutras 3.16, 3.22: Through yoga you can attain special abilities to tell the past and future.
- Sutras 3.25, 3.32: Through yoga you can discover new spirits and communicate with master spirits.
- Sutras 3.17, 3.38: Powers of sorcery can be attained through yogic meditation practice.
- Sutras 3.5: By mastering yogic meditation, you can become omniscient. (In other words, become a god)

3. Does the "Christian Yoga instructor" teach the eight limbs of yoga based on Patañjali's writings?

If so, it's Occultism and Hinduism.

One of the most difficult books I've ever read was *The Yoga System of Patañjali* translated from the original Sanskrit by James Haughton Woods, Professor of Philosophy at Harvard University, CAMBRIDGE, MASSACHUSETTS, University Press 1914.[281]

Reading Patañjali's work was laborious and burdensome. But I felt that if I were to be a credible researcher, I'd have to take on this difficult task. It was completely different than reading God's Word which is full of light, hope, and understanding.

Psalm 119:130 (NLT)
The teaching of your word gives light, so even the
simple can understand.

I will highlight some of Patañjali's doctrines and beliefs here.

- Patañjali taught: Yoga can propel you to "A special kind of Self." (Book 1, page 50)
- Patañjali taught that through yoga you can possess omniscience (Book 1, pages 55-56)
- Patañjali taught the pose to the "Tube" of Brahma (Book 1, page 75)
- Patañjali taught Yoga will give you progress to "Higher Stages" (Book 3, page 206)
- Patañjali promised supernormal insight through yoga (Book 3, page 206) Sound familiar? See Genesis 3:1-6
- Patañjali taught reincarnation, not resurrection (Book 3, page 247)
- Patañjali taught polytheism and groups of yoga gods (Book 3, page 256)
- Patañjali again taught how to become omniscient through yoga (Book 3, page 261)
- Patañjali taught how to penetrate into the bodies of others (Book 3, page 266)
- Patañjali taught how to become a god through yoga asanas, breathing properly, and meditations (Book 3, page 283)
- Patañjali promised invitations from principalities in high places (Book 3, page 286)
- Patañjali taught that enough Yoga allows you

213

to pass into another body and gain supernormal powers (Book 4, page 300)

WHAT DO CHRISTIAN YOGA INSTRUCTORS TEACH?

It would be prudent for every Christian to check
with a true spiritual leader before getting involved in any
questionable practice. Most who became involved in any
type of yoga probably did not check with their Spirit-filled
pastor or a solid Christian leader first. It would be wise to
bring the literature from the group trying to recruit them
and allow the spiritual leader to prayerfully discern the
spirit behind it.

> **Psalm 37:30 (NLT)**
> The godly offer good counsel; they teach right
> from wrong.

Ask serious questions. Your spiritual future, your calling,
your destiny, and your future are at stake.

ASK SERIOUS QUESTIONS

Does the "Christian Yoga" instructor teach about the
"Eight Limbs of Yoga" by Patañjali? All of the Christian
Yoga teachers I've researched do. Unfortunately, those who
get involved in some Christian brand of Yoga, thinking they
are only exercising, may have a consequential awakening in
their future.

I've learned over the years that many Christians do not
understand the spirit realm and how it affects their lives
and their future. They have no idea what gateways they are
opening to the demonic realm over their lives and their
families.

214

Did your yoga teacher instruct you in the half spinal twist? Bet you weren't told about its origin or the genesis of Hatha Yoga. Half Spinal Twist, also known as "Lord of Fish" or "Matsyendrasana" is named for the Hindu "guru and medieval co-founder of Hatha Yoga who learned the secrets of Tantric yoga and occult arts while in a fish's belly."[282]

Does the "Christian Yoga instructor" use more Sanskrit terminology than biblical terminology? Does he or she mix the two as co-equals? Does the instructor use terms like:

Asanas?	Pratyahara?
Pranayama?	Niyamas?
Eight Limbs of Yoga?	Yamas?
Samadhi?	Bandha?
Dharana?	Vinyasa?
Dhyana?	Kundalini?
Chakras?	

If so, it's likely occult or Hindu in disguise.

Ezekiel 22:26 (NLT)
Your priests have violated my instructions and defiled my holy things. They make no distinction between what is holy and what is not.

Does the Christian Yoga teacher use the same old crumbling talking points as the New Age Yoga instructors teach? If so, it's probably occult-like propaganda and half-truths.

"Yoga is a beautiful and ancient gift from God."

"Yoga is not a religion."

215

"Yoga is available for any religion."
"Yoga can deepen your faith."
"Yoga helps your connection with God."
"You can re-intention yoga to fit your Christianity."
The three top Christian Yoga promoters are Nancy Roth (*An Invitation to Christian Yoga*), Susan Bordenkircher (*Yoga for Christians: A Christ-Centered Approach to Physical and Spiritual Health*), and Brooke Boon (*Holy Yoga— Exercise for the Christian Body and Soul*). I have read from each of these three authors. They seem like good people, and I don't doubt that. Nonetheless, all of them carry a syncretistic theology; a blending of Christian beliefs with Hindu occult-like practices.

Just a couple of years ago another author broke onto the scene, Susan Neal (Scripture Yoga: 21 Bible Lessons for Christian Yoga Classes). I have not reviewed her material yet.

MORE QUESTIONS

Does the "Christian Yoga instructor" teach any of the 150 yoga poses that were copyrighted by the Hindu Indian Government? If so, they are teaching "stolen yoga," and hiding behind the New Age cliché that "no religion owns yoga."

Deuteronomy 32:20 (NLT)
He said, 'I will abandon them; then see what becomes of them. For they are a twisted generation, children without integrity.

Does the yoga teacher tell you the real purpose of yoga poses and breathing exercises?

Bill Wong of "Seek God's Truth"[283]writes, "The actions in yoga (breathing, movements, hand and body positions, etc.) are specifically designed to manipulate your body and mind. It is meant to prepare the body and mind by changing the energy within (manipulating your 'energy centers' called 'chakras')"

Yoga is not just a harmless exercise. Doing only the physical postures in yoga will alter you mentally and spiritually, leaving you entirely open and defenseless against the dark enemy forces from the spirit realm. It slowly guides you away from the One True God of the Bible.

Bill continues, "Yoga is trying to yoke you with the enemy. This is why all people—even Christians—must steer clear from yoga at all costs."[284]

STILL MORE QUESTIONS

- What are the Christian qualifications for Christian brand yoga teachers?
- Do they teach the fundamentals of the Christian faith, or do they just teach yoga?
- They say they are "preachers of the gospel" so, where were they trained as preachers, and who trained them?
- Do they give invitations for people to come to Jesus Christ in their public meetings?
- Since they call it "Christian Yoga," what are the purity standards for their teachers (This includes all Christian Yoga brands)?

If you are a teacher anointed by God, you have a unique

gift. My prayer is that you won't waste it on "wood, hay, and stubble" but teach God's Word for what it says, not for what you want it to say. I pray that Jesus Christ will be pre-eminent in your life and that the Holy Spirit will help you teach godliness and truth to your students. If you are teaching a pagan doctrine, I pray that the strong gift of discerning of spirits will bring you to repent and turn your life around.

America is now experiencing a demonic invasion disguised as something else. I ask God to make you the one who exposes it and, using your authority as a Christ-follower, to stop it, not perpetuate it. Be the amazing hero you were meant to be and stand only for biblical truth.

Proverbs 9:9 (NLT)
Instruct the wise, and they will be even wiser. Teach the righteous, and they will learn even more.

If you read, study, and meditate on God's Word you will clearly understand that yoga is a pagan practice and there is no way to biblically justify it.

Psalm 86:11(NLT)
Teach me your ways, O LORD, that I may live according to your truth! Grant me purity of heart, so that I may honor you.

Just as the Bible teaches about counterfeit Jesuses, it also tells us about a counterfeit Holy Spirit. You'll be shocked as you learn about him next.

21
CHAPTER

THE COUNTERFEIT
HOLY SPIRIT OF YOGA

Squandering the Future for Today's Delusion

*Now may the God of hope fill you with all joy
and peace in believing, so that you may abound in
hope, through the power of the Holy Spirit.*
~ Romans 15:13 MEV

Can you imagine how a husband would feel if he discovered that his wife was involved in, and enjoying a sexual encounter with another man? I suppose, if he is a typical, normal man, he would feel devastated, crushed, betrayed, and deeply wounded. The unfaithfulness of a spouse, God tells us, compares to spiritual adultery.[285]

I wonder how God feels when His bride commits spiritual adultery with pagan deities that are categorically identified as demons.[286]

John received some powerful revelations from God while he was on the Island of Patmos. The Holy Spirit showed this Apostle of Love that in the last days before Christ's return, sadly, people will not repent and turn to God, but will continue to worship these types of demons.[287]

In fact, the Lord later showed the apostle a world-class city that becomes a home for demonic creatures and a hideout for every foul spirit. Something apparently will open enough portals to the dark demonic realm that will cause the entire city to collapse in one hour.[288]

Could it be that just as Germany opened her doors to the dark realm when yoga spread as a popular craze, and Adolph Hitler became Chancellor, that this future city will similarly open satanic gateways, attracting demons and foul spirits that will lead to its disastrous downfall?

God warned his people that the whole land would become defiled and polluted if they chose to follow the customs of the pagan nations (Ezekiel 33:3-6; 36:16-22). The very first Commandment strictly forbids God's people from involvement with other gods. There apparently would be some kind of strange and perhaps preternatural attraction to these other gods, and that's likely the reason the Lord warned His people not to go after or chase them—to prevent a curse from coming on them and their families.[289]

Exodus 20:3 NKJV
"You shall have no other gods before Me.

Deuteronomy 6:14 NKJV
You shall not go after other gods, the gods of the
peoples who are all around you

JOHN SAW THINGS TO COME

By revelation of the Holy Spirit, the Apostle John
actually saw the things to come on the earth in the last days.

John 16:13 (NKJV)
[13] However, when He, the Spirit of truth, has
come, He will guide you into all truth; for He
will not speak on His own *authority,* but whatever He hears He will speak; and He will tell you
things to come.

WHO IS THE REAL HOLY SPIRIT?

The Holy Spirit is God's personal presence on the
earth. The Holy Spirit is God; a Person and not merely a
force. Jesus taught the disciples that the Holy Spirit would
"convict the world of guilt in regard to sin and righteousness
and judgment" (John 16:7-11).

Once we join God's family by turning from our sin and
receiving Jesus Christ, the Holy Spirit comes to live in us,
sealing us as His children (Romans 8:9; 1 Corinthians 6:19-
20, 12:13). Jesus told the disciples that the Spirit would be
our Helper, Comforter, and Guide (John 14:16). The Holy
Spirit is your Friend who always has your best interest at
heart. He speaks to you, guides you, warns you, loves you,
and always desires the best for you. He is God.

The anointing of the Holy Spirit on your life will always
lead to Truth; never to a counterfeit.

Luke 11:11-13 (NKJV)
[11] If a son asks for bread from any father among you, will he give him a stone? Or if he asks for a fish, will he give him a serpent instead of a fish?

[12] Or if he asks for an egg, will he offer him a scorpion?

[13] If you then, being evil, know how to give good gifts to your children, how much more will your heavenly Father give the Holy Spirit to those who ask Him!"

The Holy Spirit will never give you a serpent if you ask for a fish. And the Holy Spirit will never lead you into a "serpent religion" like yoga.

Just as Paul warned, there are those who choose to chase after, promote, and worship bogus gods, fraudulent saviors, and counterfeit Holy Spirits.[290]

Now, why do I point out the satanic nature of the yoga system? There are people I love that "do yoga." I know Christians who are involved in the pagan practice and attempting to integrate Christianity with paganism. I am not being judgmental or mean-spirited, but trying to save them from the heartache ahead for themselves and their families. I am a watchman, but not a watchdog.

Ezekiel 33:3-6 (NLT)
[3] When the watchman sees the enemy coming, he sounds the alarm to warn the people.

[4] Then if those who hear the alarm refuse to take action, it is their own fault if they die.

[5] They heard the alarm but ignored it, so the responsibility is theirs. If they had listened to the warning, they could have saved their lives.

> [6] But if the watchman sees the enemy coming and doesn't sound the alarm to warn the people, he is responsible for their captivity. They will die in their sins, but I will hold the watchman responsible for their deaths.'

I have heard and read remarks from those who believe yoga is a totally acceptable practice for Christians. I am not angry with them but I pity them because deception is corrupting their souls. Satan's filthy claws are scratching away at their once bright future.

I read the cheap and sarcastic comments against Matt Walsh, a writer at the Daily Wire, when he made a post about yoga saying, "Yoga Is a Pagan Ritual. Maybe Christians Should Find a Different Workout Routine."[291]

SOME OF THE COMMENTS WENT SOMETHING LIKE THIS:

"I did yoga once. Three years later my neighbor's dog died. I shouldn't have done yoga."

"My cousin did yoga. She ended up growing six arms."

Others commented that it's perfectly okay to practice yoga if you name it something else.

"Yoga is a form of exercise that has positive effects on the body physically, mentally, and emotionally. It's only a pagan ritual if you make it one. If it really bothers you, just call it stretching."

Obviously, that comment was from someone unfamiliar with the Bible. *You cannot change the nature of something simply by changing the name.* You can call Leviathan "Levi" if you want, but it will not change the hideous demonic being that it is.

And here was a comment from a strong, wise, and mature believer:

"I've always had a check in my spirit about yoga. Thanks for sharing your research and assertions! And I love reading all points of view from all different types of sources. But at the end of the day, as a Christian, the Bible is my plumb line."

WHEN PEOPLE DISCOVERED WHAT I WAS WRITING

It's amazing. When people found out I was writing articles and commentaries about Christian-brands of Yoga and possibly an entire book, I started getting letters, e-mails, tweets, and comments. Some were sent by older Christians that sounded as though they had never been taught the fundamentals of the faith. I was stunned by some of their comments and personal opinions.

St. Paul did warn us that a day would finally come that would lead to a great apostasy when "people will no longer listen to sound and wholesome teaching. They will follow their own desires and will look for teachers who will tell them whatever their itching ears want to hear.[292]

> **Revelation 9:21**
> Neither repented they of their murders, nor of their sorceries, nor of their fornication, nor of their thefts.

AN APPOINTMENT WITH KUNDALINI

One of the Devil's counterfeits for the Holy Spirit is known as "the kundalini spirit." The kundalini spirit encountered in Christian Yoga classes seems to give the students an unusual peace, ecstasy, sometimes a "prophetic word," and often feelings of euphoria, intervals of tremendous joy, love, peace and compassion. Some describe intense and explosive forms of energy flooding their bodies. They have no idea where that "energy" comes from.

The students may actually believe they are having an encounter with the real Holy Spirit. They trust their feelings; their emotions, instead of God's Word. They, without realizing it, may be making an appointment with the kundalini spirit who wishes to draw them into deeper deception. That's why I keep repeating this: discernment is our lifeline (Hebrews 5:14).

Proverbs 14:15 MSG
The gullible believe anything they're told; the prudent sift and weigh every word.

I'm not suggesting that the Christian brand Yoga teachers are intentionally leading their students into false Holy Spirit encounters. They simply lack spiritual maturity and spiritual discernment by trusting feelings over the Word of God. If you listen to the testimonies of the women involved in the Christian-brand Yoga classes, you'll find almost all of them speak of their feelings; how yoga makes them feel. It seems that it's all about feelings rather than Truth.

If you have ever read the *Yoga Sutras of Patañjali* (as I have), you realize that yoga is related entirely to divination and sorcery. Satan is an expert in how to attract and relentlessly pull his victims into deeper levels of darkness, while convincing them that God is doing it all. And all the Christian-brand Yoga teachers I've read are teaching the "Eight Limbs of Yoga" by Patañjali. That's disturbing. They seem to venerate a historical sorcerer, which is precisely what Patañjali was.

Jeremiah 14:14 NKJV
And the Lord said to me, "The prophets prophesy lies in My name. I have not sent them, commanded them, nor spoken to them; they prophesy to you a false vision, divination, a worthless thing, and the deceit of their heart.

Revelation 18:23 NKJV
...by your sorcery all the nations were deceived.

2 Timothy 3:5-7 NKJV
[5] having a form of godliness but denying its power. And from such people turn away!

[6] For of this sort are those who creep into households and make captives of gullible women loaded down with sins, led away by various lusts,

[7] always learning and never able to come to the knowledge of the truth.

Would you agree that yoga teachers could qualify as being highlighted in the above Scriptures?

In the next chapter, we will delve into more about kundalini, a kundalini awakening, and the consequences.

22

THE KUNDALINI
AWAKENING

Is Yoga a Pathway into Forbidden Sorcery?

And do not grieve the Holy Spirit of God, in
whom you are sealed for the day of redemption.
~ Ephesians 4:30 MEV

Every time you see the word "sorcery" in the Bible, you could replace it with the word "yoga" and not do any injustice to God's Word since yoga is a practice in sorcery. Again, Patañjali's Yoga Sutras (The "Eight Limbs" taught by yoga instructors) are very clear about the true path and purpose of yoga: to lead the practitioner to sorcery-type of occult experiences such as astral projection, invitations from "higher beings," psychic abilities, knowledge of past lives, and reincarnation.

I encourage you to listen to Jessica Smith's testimony,

a former yoga instructor and Reiki master. She sincerely believed she was really helping people. Then she discovered in a shattering way that she actually was guiding them into the treacherous realm of the demonic.

You can listen to Jessica's amazing testimony on Understanding the Times Radio with Jan Markell. The broadcast title was, "Warning: When the East Seduces the Church" published on 27 October 2018.[293]

I encourage you to read Jessica's web page, The Truth Behind Yoga.[294] (www.thetruthbehindyoga.com.) Get a copy of her book, *The Shattering: An Encounter With Truth*.[295]

You may also want to listen to Dr. David Reagan's interview with the late Caryl Matrisciana, filmmaker and producer of "Yoga Uncoiled", which looks at how this pagan practice has invaded the Church. You may be interested in seeing her interview with Dr. Reagan entitled, "Christian Yoga Uncoiled" with Dr. David Reagan and Caryl Matrisciana.[296]—(http://christinprophecy.org/sermons/matrisciana-on-christian-yoga/)

THE REAL INTENTION OF ANY BRAND OR TYPE OF YOGA

The real purpose of yoga, along with its unique poses, is to gently lead the participant to a "spiritual awakening." Unfortunately, that does not mean a Holy Spirit awakening but an activation of the kundalini spirit, a satanic counterfeit of the Holy Spirit. This experience, according to the yoga sutras, can lead to supernatural abilities such as clairvoyance and other blasts of occult powers connected to divination and sorcery.

Ezekiel 13:6 (NKJV)
They have envisioned futility and false divination, saying, 'Thus says the LORD!' But the LORD has not sent them; yet they hope that the word may be confirmed.

Acts 16:16 (TPT)
[16] One day, as we were going to the house of prayer, we encountered a young slave girl who had an evil spirit of divination, the spirit of Python. She had earned great profits for her owners by being a fortune-teller.

A kundalini awakening or a similar demonic intrusion can be triggered *unintentionally* while performing yoga poses, doing mindful (or contemplative) Eastern-type meditations, along with pranayama (breathing exercises) regardless of the background music or on what or whom you are meditating.

An increasing number of discerning pastors are warning that the kundalini spirit is invading the Church. Recently, Pastor John Lindell of James River Assembly of God issued a stern but loving warning to his congregation about the spiritual hidden dangers of yoga. [297]

Pastor Jonas Clark, another respected minister issued a strong warning to Christians who may lean toward thinking yoga is neutral. He said,

"Yoga is conditioning a new generation and becoming acceptable, offered as a means for weight loss, mental clarity, physical fitness and a harmless path to inner peace and harmony. Even schools are buying Yoga mats, promoting 'Yoga Ed' and exposing our nations' children to its demonic deception. Today everything is acceptable in the public square except Christianity. Yes, Yoga is a demonic teaching that is sweeping the country." [298]

YOGA AND SORCERY

Yoga is a form of sorcery and divination, plain and simple. Apostle Paul found himself dealing with a sorcerer, and called him "son of the devil" saying he was filled with every form of fraud and deceit. That describes yoga.

> **Acts 13:9-10 (TPT)**
> [9] Saul, also known as Paul, stared into his eyes and rebuked him. Filled with the Holy Spirit, he said,
>
> [10] "You son of the devil! You are full of every form of fraud and deceit and an enemy of all that is right. When will you stop perverting the truth of God into lies?

> **Deuteronomy 5:9 (NLT)**
> [9] You must not bow down to them or worship them, for I, the LORD your God, am a jealous God who will not tolerate your affection for any other gods. I lay the sins of the parents upon their children; the entire family is affected—even children in the third and fourth generations of those who reject me.

Researcher Bruce Greyson M.D., Professor Emeritus of Psychiatry and Neurobehavioral Sciences at the University of Virginia, reported that this [a kundalini awakening] "can cause major disruptions to psychological functioning that resemble psychiatric disorders and often result in a misdiagnosis of mental illness. Other researchers note that it can also cause physical problems, including involuntary spasms and vibrations, burning or itching sensations, and lethargy. People may hear voices, see visions of light and have psychic experiences."[299]

OCCULT EXPERIENCE: THE "IMPLICIT PURPOSE OF YOGA"

Dr. Greyson's term for this is the "Physio-Kundalini Syndrome." Dr. Greyson wrote, "Eastern traditions have developed elaborate lifelong practices and lifestyles with the intent of awakening kundalini; this is, in fact, the implicit purpose of yoga."[300]

I obtained a fascinating book by Ben Snyder about the deliverance ministry of Dean Hochstetler. I found it compelling to read, as this Spirit-filled Mennonite minister meticulously recorded his case studies in dealing with the demonic from 1974 to 2005.

Snyder compiled and edited Hochstetler's case studies on deliverance. I know of very few deliverance ministers that ever bothered to take both a spiritual and scientific approach to demonism the way Hochstetler did. Snyder, in his book, *The Ministry of Dean Hochstetler 1974-2005*, records the findings, case reports, discoveries, and patterns of identifying demonic practices of sorcery, of which yoga is a part, and their consequences.

According to Hochstetler, "The effects of this type of practice are serious and there are consequences." He goes on to list some of these consequences he observed in his ministry:[301]

Spiritual blindness is listed first. Then there comes a lack of assurance of salvation and a blockage to the authentic gifts of the Holy Spirit.

Physically, Hochstetler noticed that those involved faced constant sicknesses and sometimes serious diseases. He recorded that deformed, lame, or mentally impaired children were born in the generational line to those who were practicing types of sorcery. Eventually, immorality occurs, and demons began to visit the household regularly.

Hochstetler also pointed out that in his years he has seen strict church discipline for trivial issues, but has never once seen church discipline for sorcery practices [like yoga]. He goes on to say that the sins of idolatry are mentioned over 500 times in over 1,200 verses! So this seems to be one of the biggest issues (if not the biggest issue) in the Bible. According to 1 Corinthians 10:20 it mentions that behind an idol is a demonic power.[302]

WHO OR WHAT IS KUNDALINI?

Kundalini is a demon spirit known as the counterfeit Holy Spirit. The concept actually comes from Eastern religions, is activated through yoga postures, Eastern meditation techniques, and is incorporated into New Age philosophies and practices.

Mystics from the Eastern world have always referred to the expression, "Awakening the Kundalini." New Agers and Hindu gurus teach about a serpent spirit that resides in

232

each person like a coiled snake at the base of the spine. Yoga instructors teach that through yoga postures, pranayama, and Eastern-style meditation, you can begin to uncoil the serpent spirit and get it to rise up your spine through seven energy points (chakras). The idea is to raise the kundalini spirit (the serpent) through all seven chakras located along the spine, until it finally reaches the crown chakra located above the top of your head.

THE SEVEN OCCULT "CHAKRAS" OR "ENERGY POINTS"

1. The Root Chakra (Muladhara) – Occultists teach that this energy point governs your feelings of survival and sense of belonging.

2. The Sacral or Pelvic Chakra (Svadhisthana) – Hindus, New Agers, Sorcerers, and Yoga Instructors will tell you this chakra is related to your sexual organs.

3. The Navel Chakra (Manipura) – This is said to be the chakra of self-esteem and confidence.

4. Heart Chakra (Anahata) – The claim is that when you stimulate this chakra, you can heal past wounds and learn to love unconditionally.

5. Throat Chakra (Vishuddha) – When this chakra is open and stimulated, according to the yoga teachers, your voice actually moves through space and you can then communicate your emotions in healthy ways.

6. Third-Eye Chakra (Anja) – This chakra allegedly

opens your mind and helps you to become unattached to logic and to receive special insights and wisdom, sort of a sixth sense. Opening the sixth chakra helps open your mind to different perspectives. Do you see the inherent danger here? This is what some New Agers call the *"Psychic opening."*

7. Crown Chakra (Sahasrara) – The crown chakra is not located in the body itself but actually hovers above the crown of the head like an aura. *This is the chakra that opens you to the spiritual realm and makes you ready for a new consciousness.*

Those who have "raised the kundalini" describe it as a mind-blowing experience.

Under the influence of this demonic spirit, victims will testify to having deep spiritual experiences, new psychic abilities, and full-body feelings of bliss and ecstasy. Those who reach the kundalini awakening often experience uncontrollable reactions such as crying, laughing, jerking, visions, trances, and sometimes insanity.

There is even a "Wiki How" webpage, complete with pictures, that shows you how to get to the kundalini awakening. Among the tips, one is to chant, "Bum Ba' Hum Mum...Yum Rum Lum." Some of the pictures are quite amusing.[303]

WHAT ARE THE SYMPTOMS OF A KUNDALINI AWAK-ENING?

The signs and symptoms of Kundalini Awakening can be different for each individual. According to those who have researched these experiences, signs, and symptoms can include:[304]

1. Energetic sensations like electricity in the body
2. Some describe internal lightning bolts
3. Shaking and jerking in the body, usually totally out of the control of the person
4. A sensation of insects or snakes crawling on the body, often along the spine
5. Feelings of cold in the body
6. Feelings of intense heat in the spine or in specific chakras
7. Spontaneous yoga postures, hand gestures, or body locks
8. Waves of intense pleasure or bliss, even leading to orgasm
9. Big emotional shifts or mood swings, well beyond the normal
10. Sensory overload—sounds, lights, noise—everything becomes overwhelming
11. Strange internal sounds that no one else can hear like buzzing, musical instruments, or thunder

12. Waves of alleged wisdom or insight

13. Heightened periods of creativity

More Reports of Kundalini Symptoms [305]

1. Feelings of becoming one with the universe

2. Non-stop energy

3. Heightened fears

4. Sensations in the private areas, spine, or head

5. Anxiety

6. Insomnia

7. Burning hot or ice cold streams moving up the spine

8. A feeling of air bubbles or snake-like movement up through the body

9. Pains in various locations throughout the body

10. Tension or stiffness of the neck, and headaches

11. A feeling of overpressure within the head

12. Vibrations, unease, or cramps in legs and other parts of the body

13. Fast pulse and increased metabolism

14. Disturbance in breathing and/or heart function

15. Sensitivity to sound, light, smell, and proximity of other people

16. Mystical/religious experiences, revelations, and/or cosmic glimpses

17. Parapsychological abilities

18. Light phenomena in or outside the body

19. Problems with finding balance between strong sexual urges, and a wish to live in sublime purity

20. Total isolation due to inability to communicate inner experiences outward

21. Experiences of demon possession and poltergeist phenomena

Does it seem to you, as it does to me, that many of the conditions yoga is supposed to cure are actually being caused by practicing yoga?

"Evil spirits such as kundalini, yoga, and occult mysticism are dangerous spirits entering Christian churches in North America. These spirits are prophetic, offer visions, dreams, and feelings of peace. They can even feel like the Holy Spirit. Only the most discerning are seeing it."
~Apostle Jonas Clark [306]

I DO YOGA?

I hear some Christians bragging, "I Do Yoga!" They proudly carry their "I Do Yoga" bags everywhere for others to see. I've never seen a Christian yogi or yogini carrying a bag that reads, "I do holiness." Nor have I seen a Christian Yoga adherent wearing a yoga top that reads, "Jesus is my Lord!" I have seen them wearing "Jesus is my Guru."

Is it possible that saying, "I Do Yoga" is actually saying...

...I do lewdness?

...I do narcissism?

...I do sorcery?

...I do occult?

...I do paganism?

...I do idolatry?

...I do a sex cult?

...I do divination?

...I do inferior exercises?

...I do what God has forbidden?

...I do rebellion?

...I do witchcraft?

...I do apostasy?

...I do feelings?

...I do demonic portals?

...I do shamanism?

...I do Hinduism?

...I do instability?

Just a thought.

DIVIDED LOYALTIES

Among Christians who practice yoga there seems to exist divided loyalties between Jesus and the sorcery of Patañjali, author of the yoga sutras. St. James described the condition this way:

James 1:6-8 NLT

[6]...Do not waver, for a person with divided loyalty is as unsettled as a wave of the sea that is blown and tossed by the wind.

[7] Such people should not expect to receive anything from the Lord.

[8] Their loyalty is divided between God and the world, and they are unstable in everything they do.

Our Scriptures assure us that those with divided loyalties are unstable and should not expect to receive anything from the Lord.

It's puzzling how people who claim to be filled with the Holy Spirit can lack discernment. Those who have come out of the occult and sorcery, like Jessica Smith, Laurette Willis, and Kirstin Baisch, can easily discern what yoga really is, its nature, and its purpose. They clearly see that yoga is totally antithetical to God's teachings.

Apologist Chris Lawson wrote an excellent article on the kundalini energy invading the Church today. "Kundalini Energy: Yoga's Power, Influence, and Occult Phenomena in the Church"[307] by Chris Lawson. You may download it here:

http://kundalinipeak.com/myresources/ebooks/
KundaliniEnergy_YogasOccultPhenomenaintheChurch.pdf

Here's a brief excerpt from Chris's article:

"Those who have escaped the world of the occult and come to the real Jesus Christ understand very clearly what is going on. On the other hand, countless people, including many in church leadership don't have a clue. Those who are ignorant of this deadly power invading the church would do well to take heed!"

"YOGA IS AN OCCULT PRACTICE"

"I must state as clearly as possible that anyone who gets involved with yoga, and kundalini energy which is the aim of all yoga, is making a very, very big mistake. No matter how committed a Christian may be, pastor or lay person alike, when a believer chooses to involve himself or herself with the world of the occult, including any and all levels of yoga practice, for 'exercise' or otherwise, very powerful spontaneous demonic manifestations can and do oftentimes occur. Many ignorant people say that yoga exercises can be separated from yoga philosophy. This simply is not true. It is a well-known fact that yoga postures/poses are the outworking of occult philosophy. Yoga is an occult practice." ~ Chris Lawson

At *News with Views*, Marsha West writes, "Authentic Christians are to stand against evil, not engage in it!"[308]

Isaiah 30:12-14 (MSG)
Therefore, The Holy of Israel says this: "Because you scorn this Message, preferring to live by injustice and shape your lives on lies, This perverse way of life will be like a towering, badly built wall That slowly, slowly tilts and shifts, and then one day, without warning, collapses—smashed to bits like a piece of pottery, smashed beyond recognition or repair, Useless, a pile of debris to be swept up and thrown in the trash.

INSANITY AND SUICIDAL THOUGHTS

In the exposé by Lawson, "Kundalini Energy: Yoga's Power, Influence and Occult Power in the Church," he says, "During rushes of kundalini energy people become overwhelmed with states of ecstatic bliss and altered states of consciousness. At times they also sink into states of incredible despair whilst feeling fear, anxiety, sadness, anger, impending insanity, and even suicidal thoughts."[309]

IS YOGA ACTUALLY A LUCIFERIAN INITIATION?

Lawson, in his inspiring message entitled, *Does Your Pastor Know that Yoga and Christianity are not Compatible?"* says, "The manifestations of Kundalini energy that come through yoga can be hazardous and have even been known to cause death. It must be remembered that Kundalini energy is demonic power masquerading as a cosmic life force."[310]

Many believers have been tricked into thinking that yoga is just relaxation and exercise. Nothing could be further from the truth. Yoga's intent is to bring the student into an altered state of consciousness. Christians who believe they're just exercising are being scooped up into a counterfeit religion.

After a kundalini awakening, a person's mind is patently altered. Some discerners, like Tex Marrs, have called the kundalini awakening, "The Luciferian Initiation."[311]

HOPE FOR THOSE WHO HAVE STRAYED

Our wonderful God! When He speaks of judgment for His people who worship as the pagans do, He always pronounces hope if the guilty will turn back to Him. I've seen many turn from yoga recently, and they have thanked me for informing them about the satanic sorcery behind it. It was like a light came on, and now they can really worship Jesus again without the kundalini interference.

If you mistakenly became involved in some so-called Christian Yoga, you can turn away now before it's too late. God loves you and will show you His favor and mercy, but you must repent and renounce this pagan practice now. Remember yoga is yoga, regardless of the name someone slaps on the front of it. Yoga is spiritual adultery and grieves the heart of the Heavenly Father. Turn from it now and expose the works of darkness.

NO LONGER CALL SOMETHING GOOD THAT IS EVIL

Isaiah 5:20 (MSG)
Doom to you who call evil good and good evil,
Who put darkness in place of light and light
in place of darkness, Who substitute bitter for
sweet and sweet for bitter!

Remember, the Canaanite religion was exactly like today's Hinduism. In India, children are sacrificed on the fires of the garbage dumps. Mark and Huldah Buntain spent their lives trying to rescue these "throw-away" babies. The Canaanites were polytheistic (many gods, just like Hinduism) and pantheistic (God is in everything). Their customs and practices were shockingly similar to Hindu customs and practices today. But our God said to His people,

Deuteronomy 18:9-12 (MSG)
When you enter the land that God, your God, is giving you, don't take on the abominable ways of life of the nations there. Don't you dare sacrifice your son or daughter in the fire. Don't practice divination, sorcery, fortunetelling, witchery, casting spells, holding séances, or channeling with the dead. People who do these things are an abomination to God. It's because of just such abominable practices that God, your God, is driving these nations out before you.

You can return to your first love now, but it's your choice. Jesus is waiting for you with open arms. A line in the sand is drawn. Will you choose the Holy Spirit or will it be the kundalini spirit?

Revelation 2:4-5 (MSG)
"But you walked away from your first love—why? What's going on with you, anyway? Do you have any idea how far you've fallen? A Lucifer fall! "Turn back! Recover your dear early love. No time to waste, for I'm well on my way to removing your light from the golden circle.

You may sometimes feel like God has abandoned you

but He has not. St. James wrote this: Draw near to God and He will draw near to you (James 4:8 NKJV).

23

GOD HAS NOT
ABANDONED YOU!

Coming Back to Jesus

But if you refuse to serve the Lord, then choose today whom you will serve. Would you prefer the gods your ancestors served beyond the Euphrates? Or will it be the gods of the Amorites in whose land you now live? But as for me and my family, we will serve the Lord.
~ Joshua 24:15 (NLT)

We are approaching the end of our journey together in discovering what yoga really is and the effect it has on people and nations. Ultimately, you will make your own decision about yoga. You will choose based on your feelings and opinions or you will choose based on God's Word. Will you try to bend God's instructions to correspond with your feelings and personal desires, or will you adjust your actions to conform to God's will?

245

IF YOU HAVE READ THIS FAR...

If you have read this far and you are involved in yoga, it's probably because God has not abandoned you. He's reaching out to you in His mercy.

One of the stages of God's judgments, if His people refuse to repent, is called the "abandonment judgment." This is when God removes His hand of protection and allows nature to take its course. In a sense, this is also a redemptive judgment, in that when a person sees their life in confusion and disarray, hopefully, they will turn from sin and back to God.

Because you've read all the way to this chapter, it shows you care about God's thoughts on the subject of yoga. You want the truth. You want to do the right thing. Maybe you knew God at one time but somehow simply lost your way. In these final chapters, I'll show you how to come back to God's love, safety, care, and protection.

It's mind-boggling to read the social media comments when you post something about yoga. People have opinions.

To me, being a Christian, the only opinion that really matters is God's.

God knows what is best for you. He loves you. He knows something you don't. His Spirit whispers the Truth to your heart, guides, leads, explains, and reveals. God is not unreasonable.

Isaiah 1:18-20 (NKJV)

[18] "Come now, and let us reason together," Says the LORD, "Though your sins are like scarlet, They shall be as white as snow; Though they are red like crimson, They shall be as wool.

246

> [19] If you are willing and obedient, You shall eat the good of the land;
>
> [20] But if you refuse and rebel, You shall be devoured by the sword"; For the mouth of the Lord has spoken.

God is not unreasonable; however, His Truth is absolute.

3 John 4
I have no greater joy than to hear that my children walk in truth.

I've done my best to give you the truth about yoga. I've shown you God's heart on the matter and referenced many contemporary experts, including those who forsook yoga and turned to Jesus. My prayer is that you will come to know the Truth, and the Truth will set you free from any adulterated theology and heresy that may end up stealing, killing, and destroying good things in your life.[312]

DIFFICULT DIALOG

Those who have practiced yoga for a while are difficult to dialogue with.

In fact I've noticed that the longer a person practices yoga the more he (or she) becomes sympathetic toward other deviant doctrines and practices. To them, everything becomes true or "sort of true" and nothing is entirely false. They see no problem with merging conflicting beliefs, religious doctrines, and spiritual systems, then, cherry-picking what they will approve, practice, and incorporate into their own lives.

Professing Christians who are actually "Hindu in practice" tolerate contradictory doctrines, polluted theologies, and divergent practices that were never condoned, prescribed or supported in either the Old or New Testament times.[313] Often they are willing to manipulate God's Word to endorse their own fusion of assorted doctrines.

Romans 1:28 (TPT)
And because they thought it was worthless to embrace the true knowledge of God, God gave them over to a worthless mind-set, to break all rules of proper conduct.

MINDSET FOR THE ANTICHRIST

This is precisely the global mindset needed for the rise of a New World Order with one magnetic leader, exactly as the biblical prophets predicted would happen in the last days. The coming one-world government and one-world conglomerate religion are being formed on earth at this very moment. Just prior to the Second Coming of Jesus Christ, a man known as the Antichrist will rule over the world governments for a short season.

Just as Jesus Christ came to earth to fulfill God's will and purposes, the Antichrist will come to do the will and purposes of Satan.

This Antichrist will be the shaman of all shamans; the sorcerer of all sorcerers; possessed and empowered by the ancient serpent, Satan himself.

And like Germany, after yoga became such a craze, it won't turn out well for the citizens of this world.

Matthew 24:21
...for then shall be great tribulation, such as was
not since the beginning of the world to this time,
no, nor ever shall be.

In the Book of Revelation we find a global ecumenical conglomerate religion that will fully support antichrist policies. John, the Revelator identifies this religious order as a "great whore" and the "Mother of all Harlots and Abominations of the Earth." The coming "Mystery Babylon" will not only include a global political structure, an international commercial system, but also a distorted, hybrid religious order.

MONGREL MODELS

This approaching religious order will boast of its tolerance of all religions and will incorporate various aspects of many religious systems into its society. This "harlot" represents the spirit of false Christianity that mixes God's Word with aberrant, twisted and heretical doctrines and practices. Why do they amalgamate various religious traditions? It's because the abominable leaders want to offer people exactly what they want in a religion.

It seems bizarre, but there is actually "Christian Wicca" now being accepted.[314] Not only that, there are practicing witches claiming to be Christians.[315] You can find several new books today on "Christian Paganism."[316] All these seem to apply the same mongrel models as the Christian Yoga brands.

TRUE OR FALSE: ONE GOD—MANY PATHS?

The Great Harlot's slogan will probably be "One God —many paths." Lee Strobel wrote an excellent article for *Christianity Today*, "Are There Many Paths to God?"[317] It's worth reading.

> **Revelation 17:5-6a (AMP)**
> [5] And on her forehead a name was written, a mystery: "BABYLON THE GREAT, THE MOTHER OF PROSTITUTES (false religions, heresies) AND OF THE ABOMINATIONS OF THE EARTH." [6] I saw that the woman was drunk with the blood of the saints (God's people), and with the blood of the witnesses of Jesus [who were martyred].

I believe yoga will play a big part in setting up the end-time stage for the coming world delusion.

> **2 Thessalonians 2:9-12**
> [9] Even him, whose coming is after the working of Satan with all power and signs and lying wonders,
>
> [10] And with all deceivableness of unrighteousness in them that perish; because they received not the love of the truth, that they might be saved.
>
> [11] And for this cause God shall send them strong delusion, that they should believe a lie:
>
> [12] That they all might be damned who believed not the truth, but had pleasure in unrighteousness.

YOGA'S ROLE IN THE END-TIME DELUSION

From the beginning, yoga has played its part in opening "portals" to the demonic realm. After all, just look at yoga's history. The earliest yoga practitioners were the primitive shamans and sorcerers.[318] They were quite common in ancient pagan cultures but forbidden amongst God's holy people.

2 Kings 17:35 NLT
"Do not worship any other gods or bow before them or serve them or offer sacrifices to them."

Jeremiah 2:11 NKJV
Has a nation changed its gods, which are not gods? But My people have changed their Glory for what does not profit.

Think about it. Can you imagine going to a sorcery practitioner or witch doctor for your annual check-up? A typical shaman would enter a trance during a ritual to practice divination, healing, contact deceased ancestors, influence weather patterns, foretell the future, or control spiritual forces. Synonyms for shaman are: sorcerer, medicine man, witch doctor, healer, and kahuna.[319]

Yoga really *is* a Shamanistic practice historically traced to ancient Siberia and India.[320] In reality, Dhamanism dates all the way back to ancient Babylon. Yoga itself is actually a form of sorcery and divination.[321]

IS YOGA REALLY A FORM OF DIVINATION?

Divination is at the heart of the occult. Yoga, a form of divination, opens spiritual portals to the dark side and spiritually weakens a person, preparing him or her for manipulations from the invisible demonic world.

Yoga was designed to increase psychic perception,

insight, intuition, and to initiate preternatural phenomena. This is exactly what the author of the Yoga Sutras, Patañjali, taught.[322] Even most of the Christian Yoga teachers today teach the eight limbs of yoga[323] as taught by Patañjali, only they hide, disguise, or ignore the occultism attached to it.[324]

Some groups today are calling for Shamanic Yoga to be a new model for healthcare.[325] Imagine that.

While traveling in his ministry, the Apostle Paul encountered a woman who operated by a spirit of divination. This lady was friendly and even promoted Paul's meetings, but something wasn't right and Paul discerned it. If you read—really read—*The Yoga Sutras*, you'll clearly see the relationship between yoga and divination. Perhaps this woman Paul encountered owned the local yoga studio. The point is, although she seemed like a sweet lady, and even wanted to advertise the apostle's ministry, she had become demonized by an evil spirit of divination. She probably didn't even know it until Paul cast that demon out of her.

> **Acts 16:16-19**
> [16] And it came to pass, as we went to prayer, a certain damsel possessed with a spirit of divination met us, which brought her masters much gain by soothsaying:
>
> [17] The same followed Paul and us, and cried, saying, These men are the servants of the most high God, which shew unto us the way of salvation.
>
> [18] And this did she many days. But Paul, being grieved, turned and said to the spirit, I command thee in the name of Jesus Christ to come out of her. And he came out the same hour.

The spiritual realm is real. Mature believers understand this. What we practice in this natural realm attracts certain things from the invisible realm. Those things, depending on what actions we are taking, can be benevolent or malevolent, good or evil.

TRANSCENDING PHYSICAL EXISTENCE

The yoga mystics still teach that man can transcend physical existence and experience his own awakening to a connection with God, becoming "one" with God, the universe, becoming god-like, or existing on whatever higher plane he believes. They teach that you can, through yoga, reach a state of consciousness called "self-realization" which is when, they claim, you attain unity with God.

Those who promote the yoga ideology often use the name of Christ as a means of worshiping their "higher self." The "god of self" requires no repentance, confession of sin, or acknowledging the substitutionary death and resurrection of Jesus for our sins (1 Corinthians 15:3–4).

Even in some "Christianized Yoga" brands, the name of Jesus is used as sort of a prop. Jesus is often viewed as a "guru" who shows you how to exalt your own inner goodness and, in so doing, connect you with either a deity or your "higher self." Some even advertise that yoga is a way to "connect with God."

But this doesn't work. It never has and never will. Jesus Christ to the genuine Christian is the preeminent Lord, not just another add-on god. In Hindu thought, Jesus is just one of many gods.

Colossians 1:18
...that in all things he might have the preeminence.

Exodus 20:3 (AMP)
"You shall have no other gods before Me."

YOGA IS NOT A NEUTRAL ACTIVITY

"Yoga is not a universal, religiously neutral practice that Christianity can be plugged into, as is being propagated. Yoga is an ancient spiritual pagan practice. The religious doctrine and the practice it outlines are completely opposed to Biblical teachings." ~Jessica Smith (Former yoga instructor and Reiki master)

Jeremiah 14:14 (NLT)
Then the Lord said, "These prophets are telling lies in my name. I did not send them or tell them to speak. I did not give them any messages. They prophesy of visions and revelations they have never seen or heard. They speak foolishness made up in their own lying hearts.

I'm a Spirit-filled, Bible-believing Christian. I love God, and I love people. Personally, I have nothing against the people who are involved in yoga, but I abhor their idolatrous practices. I'm writing this book because I do not want to see any of my Christian brothers and sisters beguiled and led astray by embracing and adopting what I now deeply believe is a seriously errant and dangerous philosophy.

This false philosophy has the power to steal, kill and destroy and lead a practitioner down a broad path *away* from the True and Living God.

If you've strayed from your loving God, you may be wondering, "How can I turn back now?" That's what I'll show you in the final chapter.

Jeremiah 3:12-14 (NLT)

¹² Therefore, go and give this message to Israel. This is what the LORD says:

"O Israel, my faithless people, come home to me again, for I am merciful. I will not be angry with you forever.

¹³ Only acknowledge your guilt. Admit that you rebelled against the LORD your God and committed adultery against him by worshiping idols under every green tree. Confess that you refused to listen to my voice. I, the Lord, have spoken!

^{14a} "Return home, you wayward children," says the LORD, "for I am your master."

God's not finished with you.

24

CHAPTER

COMING BACK TO
THE REAL JESUS

Can a Person Follow Jesus and Pantanjali Too?
Rend your heart, and not your garments;
return to the Lord your God, for He is
gracious and merciful, slow to anger, and
abounding in steadfast love; and He relents
from punishing.
~ Joel 2:13 MEV

Authentic Christians believe the Bible is the infallible, inerrant Word of God.[326]

Pagan religions and practices do not have one main religious text or set of beliefs to follow. Instead they merge many teachings by selecting a portion, perhaps from the Bible, a little more from the Sanskrit, a dash from the local guru, or any combination of an endless number of beliefs and practices.

There is no absolute truth to a person who is not committed to Jesus Christ and God's Word, the Bible.

Christians believe that Jesus Christ is God's Son, who came to earth in His incarnation.[327] That means he was unique in all of history, being 100 percent God and 100 percent man. He lived a sinless life, healed the sick, performed miracles, and even raised the dead.[328] He is the *only* way to connect with God, the Father.[329]

He was falsely accused by jealous religious leaders, whipped and nailed to a Roman cross to suffer and die for the sin of the world. After six hours of this torturous execution, He cried out, "It is finished."[330] He died and was buried.[331] Then, surprise! He rose from the dead on the third day, was seen by many, gave instructions to His apostles, and ascended back into Heaven until the Father tells Him that it is time to go get His children.

Some Hindus believe in Jesus as one of many gods but they do not give him preeminence or believe He is the Lord. Because yoga is not just physical exercise but transmits spiritual attachments as well, it is incompatible with authentic Christian worship.

Jesus did not die so that we could violate God's Laws as we please. He died so we could possess the power to follow God with all our hearts, souls, and strength. He died so we who receive Him could become sons and daughters of God; royalty, not connected by an ancient pagan practice, but connected by a new birth—a spiritual birth.[332] Along with that spiritual birth brings us forgiveness of sin,[333] a new nature,[334] and promises us a home in Heaven when our life is finished on earth.

We can only experience that re-birth by placing our faith in Jesus Christ and His finished work on our behalf. He took the rap for our sins, and we who trust Him and follow Him have received His righteousness. What a trade! He took our sins, and we took His righteousness.

When we experience the new birth, the Holy Spirit now teaches us.[335]

If you have accepted and practiced the yogic philosophy, you will find yourself at odds with God's Word and God's Spirit. As I said before, the Christian worldview and yogic worldview are antithetical to each other.

We know we cannot follow Jesus, God's perfect Son, and follow a sorcerer too. Patañjali's view of God's nature is out of harmony with God's Truth. No person can serve two masters.[336] It's either one or the other. Syncretism, as found in Christian Yoga brands, is twisted theology.

Therefore, it is my conclusion, that a true practicing Christian cannot be a follower of Jesus and practice yoga at the same time.[337] I know some try. Why? I don't know their hearts. And I don't condemn them—that's not my job. My job is to love them enough to tell them the truth about Jesus and the straightforward truth about the practice of yoga. And that's what I hope I have been able to achieve in *Yoga Craze in the Last Days.*

Probably every Christian has made some kind of bad decision along the way in their life. I have. Even St. Paul apparently made some wrong decisions during his time of ministry on earth. What must we do when we find we've chosen a false path? Repent. That simply means to turn around now and come to Jesus for mercy, forgiveness, and restoration. When you do, I'm certain God will lift you to a new place of honor because you had the courage to choose the truth over a falsehood.

Just as God honored Mike Shreve, Jessica Smith, and Kirstin Baisch with great influence and respectable ministries when they renounced yoga and chose to follow the *real* Jesus, He will do the same for you.

CHRISTIANS SHOULD BE CREATIVE

Christians should be the most creative people on earth. After all, the Holy Spirit lives in us, and He, along with the Father and the Son, is the Creator.

Why would Christians have to use old worn-out exercises when the One who created us is willing to show us creative exercises that honor Jesus rather than Shiva?

If some of the Christian Yoga teachers got together, repented of their Scripture-twisting, set up a few prayer meetings to seek the Lord, and determined to follow only Jesus Christ without the Hindu add-on of yoga, I wouldn't be surprised if they came up with a new exercise that spread throughout the world like wildfire. They would probably become influential and generous millionaires, connected to the heart of God and to the Great Commission.

I understand. It really is difficult to admit when we've been wrong about something. But it sure is worth it, since promotion only comes from the Lord (Psalm 75:6-7).

Do you want your life, your business, or your ministry to enjoy God's promotion? Come back completely to Jesus now. He's waiting without censure or judgment to embrace you in a supernatural way and let you know how much He loves you. Jesus and you will make a great partnership in your next venture. And when He has preeminence in your life, hang on! The adventure really begins now.

I encourage you to read Jessica Smith's testimony. She knew Jesus, but then turned to yoga. Then after years of leading others falsely in yoga, she had a "shattering moment" that drove her back to the loving Savior. I know Jessica would love it if you read her book, *The Shattering — An Encounter with Truth*.[338] You can find it on Amazon or at Jessica's web page store: https://www.truthbehindyoga.com.

We've all sinned and fallen short of God's glory and standards.

Romans 3:23 (NKJV)
...for all have sinned and fall short of the glory of God

The bad news is that one sin can keep us out of Heaven, regardless of all the good we may have done in life. If we've ever gossiped, told a lie, or even taken a pencil from our place of work, we've sinned. Since there is not enough good we could do to cover for that one sin, we are lost unless we have a Savior.

Romans 6:23
For the wages of sin is death; but the gift of God is eternal life through Jesus Christ our Lord.

God provided that Savior. He's God's Son, Jesus. There is no other way. There is no "Plan B" to get you into Heaven, to give you a new nature, and to bring you into true fellowship with God. Jesus is the only solution to the sin problem and the only way to connect with God.

Romans 10:9 (NKJV)
that if you confess with your mouth the Lord Jesus and believe in your heart that God has raised Him from the dead, you will be saved.

John 1:12 (NKJV)
But as many as received Him, to them He gave the right to become children of God, to those who believe in His name

Well, what should I do now, you may ask? It's so simple, a child can do it. You simply come to Jesus as you are; any condition, sins and all. Ask Him to forgive you and give you a new start in life. If you've followed any false ways, tell Him. Believe in your heart that Jesus died for you and that He was raised from the dead and you'll experience a new birth (John 3:3).

I would be happy to lead you in a prayer right now. You don't have to understand it all, but you do have to believe it. Let's pray this prayer together. You can read it now out loud—loud enough for your own ears to hear your words. Ready? Let's do it!

"Dear Lord Jesus, please forgive me for all my sins. Cleanse me of all the twisted things I've thought, said and done that were offensive to You. I'm really sorry. I believe You died on the cross for me, and that You were raised from the dead. I declare with my mouth that You are my Lord, and I receive You as my Savior and my only hope of ever having a home in Heaven.

If anything evil and not of You has joined me, take it from me now. Fill me with Your Spirit and teach me to love Your Word and hear the voice of Your Spirit. Thank you, Lord Jesus. I'm forgiven. I have a new nature implanted within me. I have a home in heaven waiting for me, and I have a brand new start in life beginning NOW. Amen!"

If you really meant it when you prayed that prayer, Jesus hit the clear button on your "sin calculator" in Heaven. Now there's nothing but a big "ZERO" on it. Also the angels in heaven are rejoicing.[339] Not only that, your name is ringing out throughout Heaven and the population there is so happy you've come (or returned) to Jesus Christ.[340] Tell someone right away that you prayed with me and that Jesus is now your Lord.

I'd love to give you a free download of my best-selling book, *The New Life—The Start of Something Wonderful.*

You can find it here: www.DaveWilliams.com/NL

I know you now have a great future. I'm certain that Jesus will be with you all through your life, walking with you hand-in-hand.[341]

FAITH BUILDING PRODUCTS

CRASH COURSE IN INTERCESSORY PRAYER
(MP3 INSTANT DOWNLOAD)

God is looking for a few good men and women! He needs powerful prayer warriors to join his elite team of intercessors. Prayer moves mountains, changes circumstances, and touches God's heart.

These messages, by Dr. Dave Williams will help you develop your prayer "muscles" so your prayers bring down blessings from heaven and destroy every snare of the enemy!

Become a more powerful, anointed intercessor!

Release the Dynamic Power of Prayer in Your Life

- Message 1: Motivation for Intercessory Prayer
- Message 2: Intercessory Prayer and Fasting
- Message 3: Intercessory Prayer and Spiritual Gifts

DAVEWILLIAMS.COM/STORE

DEFEATING THE REALM OF THE DEMONIC
(MP3 INSTANT DOWNLOAD)

There is more to this life than what is visible to the human eye. There is a spiritual realm of demonic beings bent on killing and destroying lives and stealing what rightfully belongs to you. But there is good news! If Jesus is your Savior, you have power in you that is greater than any other power in the world! Jesus has given you the authority to cast out demons and live a life free of demonic influences. It is time that you—as a believer—begin to exercise that God-given power.

Sessions Include

- Session 1: Defeating the Realm of the Demonic
- Session 2: The Effect of Demonic Influence
- Session 3: How Demons Get a Foothold
- Session 4: Common Symptoms of Demonic Involvement
- Session 5: Discerning of Spirits

NEXT LEVEL FASTING
(MP3 INSTANT DOWNLOAD)

Fasting, coupled with prayer, is one of the most powerful spiritual combinations on earth! These messages share 32 important things about fasting God wants YOU to know, principles that can open the door to success in your life! Next Level Fasting will unlock God's power in your life. When you are obedient to fast, as Jesus did, your faith will grow exponentially and you will be blessed.

Why is Fasting & Prayer Important?

Fasting and Prayer is a time to disrupt our schedules and declare that God is more important and essential than anything else that vies for our time. Fasting is one of the most powerful yet least understood weapons in the believer's arsenal.

- Message 1: What God Wants You to Know About Fasting – Part 1
- Message 2: What God Wants You to Know About Fasting – Part 2
- Message 3: What is Fasting?
- Message 4: The Purpose and Proper Attitudes for Fasting
- Message 5: Rewards for Fasting

DAVEWILLIAMS.COM/STORE

SUPERNATURAL GIFTS OF THE HOLY SPIRIT
(MP3 INSTANT DOWNLOAD)

A Crash Course in Personality and Charismatic Gifts of the Holy Spirit

Do you need a solution? Are you tired of sitting on the sidelines of life? God has not left you alone; he sent you his Holy Spirit to come along side and help you. God has imparted in each of us, Kingdom Gifts of the Holy Spirit.

This powerful four-part series is the play book to discovering, developing, and deploying your gifts. In these lessons Dr. Dave coaches you on the biblical truths of seven personality gifts and nine gifts.

As you listen, you will discover the benefits of identifying your gifts and learn how to honor God's supernatural power in your life.

- Message 1: Personality Gifts
- Message 2: Charismatic Gifts: Part 1
- Message 3: Charismatic Gifts: Part 2
- Message 4: Charismatic Gifts: Part 3

DAVEWILLIAMS.COM/STORE

24 REASONS TO AVOID YOGA: IF YOU ARE A CHRISTIAN
(AMAZON & KINDLE)

For those who want to warn others about Yoga in a succinct manner, we've produced a book with exerpts and commentary on the comprehensive book, *Yoga Craze in the Last Days.* Dr. Dave Williams takes you on a journey he never wanted to take—a journey into the world of deception and delusion. Most Christians have no idea what Yoga really is, and what it can do to their lives and family.

- Is Yoga the greatest fraud ever perpetrated against American women?
- Does Christian-style Yoga attract a strong delusion?
- Are Yoga-related injuries on the rise...including strokes?
- Does Yoga carry and transmit a certain spirit?
- Does Yoga really open demonic gateways into your life, family, and future?
- Did God warn His people about mixing pagan practices into their faith?

Find out as you read...*24 Reasons to Avoid Yoga if You are a Christian.*

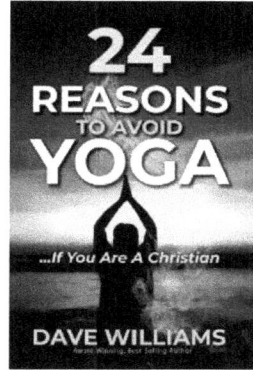

ENDNOTES

1. Cumby, Constance. The Hidden Dangers of the Rainbow: The New Age Movement and Our Coming Age of Barbarism. Huntington House. 1983. ISBN-13: 978-0910311038

2. Groothuis, Douglas R. Unmasking the New Age. InterVarsity Press. 1986. ISBN13:9780877845683

3. Springfield News-Sun https://www.springfieldnewssun.com/news/national/pastor-warns-about-demonic-roots-yoga-teacher-called-remarks-ludicrous/5SPBTPK2rC8EMvefs0gWNP/ (Accessed 01/28/2019)

4. https://www.christianpost.com/news/christian-witch-claims-christ-followers-can-practice-witchcraft-despite-biblical-warnings.html (Accessed 01/26/2019)

5. https://christianwicca.org/ (Accessed 01/03/2019)

6. https://www.amazon.com/Melanie-Christian-Mediums-Gifts-Spirit-ebook/dp/B015269SP4 (Accessed 12/28/2018)

7. https://www.psychicguild.com/readings/christian (Accessed 12/27/2018)

8. http://www.christianspracticingyoga.com/ (Accessed 01/04/2019)

9. 1 Timothy 4:1 NKJV

10. The Yoga System Of Patañjali, translated from the original Sanskrit by James Haughton Woods, Professor of Philosophy at Harvard University, CAMBRIDGE, MASSACHUSETTS, University Press 1914.

11. http://seekgodstruth.com/sotdangersofyoga.html (Accessed 01/05/2019)

12. Matthew 24:4, 5, 11; Romans 16:18; 1 Corinthians 15:33; Colossians 2:4; 2 Thessalonians 2:3; 1 John 2:26; 3:7

13. 2 Thessalonians 2:10-13

14. 1 Timothy 4:1; 2 Thessalonians 2:3

15. "Beloved, do not believe every spirit, but test the spirits, whether they are of God. (1 John 4:1)

16. https://holyyoga.net/about/what-we-believe/ (Accessed 06/15/2-18)

17. https://holyyoga.net/

18. Got Questions? What is Holy Yoga? (https://www.gotquestions.org/holy-yoga.html)

19. Indo-Aryans of ancient India

20. New Dimension in Vedic Occultism (A Treatise in Vedanga Jyotisha) Paperback – 2000 by Bepin Behari (Author)

21. Christian Yoga: An Oxymoron? by Marcia Montenegro/Christian Answers for the New Age

22. https://www.youtube.com/watch?v=iKtJLe5PAco (Accessed 05/07/2019)

23. https://www.yogadangers.com/wheaton-college-featured-in-dr-candy-gunther-browns-presidential-address-to-the-american- society-of-church-history-video-christian-yoga-something-new-under-the-sun-son/

24. http://www1.cbn.com/700club/should-christians-do-yoga (Should Christians Do Yoga?) (Retrieved 06/03/2018)

25. https://praisemoves.com/ (Retrieved 06/03/2018)

26. http://www1.cbn.com/700club/should-christians-do-yoga (Retrieved 06/03/2018)

27. HinduismToday.com – 9/13/09 Professor Subhas Tiwari of Hindu University of America, (Accessed 06/01/2018)

28. http://www.dictionary.com/browse/yoga?s=t (Accessed 06/01/2018)

29. https://albertmohler.com/2010/09/20/the-subtle-body-should-christians-practice-yoga/ (Accessed 06/01/2018)

30. https://s3-us-west-2.amazonaws.com/hy-website/YogaandChrist.pdf (Retrieved 06/04/2018)

31. 1 Corinthians 5:6; Galatians 5:9

32. 2 Corinthians 11:4 For if he who comes preaches another Jesus whom we have not preached, or if you receive a different spirit which you have not received, or a different gospel which you have not accepted—you may well put up with it!

33. http://www.spiritual-research-network.com/christianyogahinduoccult_pt1.html (Retrieved 06/12/2018)

34. Matthew 24:4, 5, 11; Romans 16:18; 1 Corinthians 15:33; Colossians 2:4; 2 Thessalonians 2:3; 1 John 2:26; 3:7

35. TM (Transcendental Meditation) is a form of yoga, and was pursued by the German Government youth department (Ministry of Youth, Family and Health), verified by the nations Supreme Courts after careful review.

36. 2 Corinthians 5:10; Hebrews 9:27: And as it is appointed unto men once to die, but after this the judgment.

37. Indo-Aryans of ancient India

38. Sanskrit: the ancient language in Hinduism. The Sanskrit was used as a means of communication and dialogue with the Hindu Celestial gods.

39. Genesis 3:5

40. http://www.christiananswersforthenewage.org/Articles_YogaHippies1.html

41. Chris Lawson http://www.spiritual-research-network.com/christianyogahin-duoccult_pt1.html (Retrieved 07/01/2018)

42. https://www.gotquestions.org/Christian-yoga.html (Accessed 0610/2018)

43. http://www.newsweek.com/christians-should-not-do-yoga-says-indian-catho-lic-church-873140 (Accessed 06/25/2018)

44. https://albertmohler.com/2010/09/20/the-subtle-body-should-christians-practice-yoga/ (Retrieved 06/25/2018)

45. http://www.spiritual-research-network.com/christianyogahinduoccult_pt1.html (Retrieved 06/10/2018)

46. http://www.doormousehouse.com/2013/10/yoga-your-christian-walk-never-twain.html (Accessed 07/01/2018)

47. https://praisemoves.com/

48. https://www.wholyfit.com/new-about-us-page

49. Ephesians 5:11 (NKJV), 1 John 1:6 (NKJV), Ephesians 4:14-16 (NKJV).

50. https://crossexamined.org/christian-apologetics/ Accessed 07/05/2018
https://answersingenesis.org/apologetics/ Accessed 07/05/2018

51. http://www.churchandgospel.com/2015/09/29/the-apostle-paul-as-christian-apologist/ Accessed 06/28/2018

52. Nelson, P.C., Bible Doctrines, ISBN-13: 9780882438580, https://www.christianbook.com/bible-doctrines-revised-75th-anniversary-edition/p-c-nel-son/9780882438580/pd/438581?en=google&event=SHOP&kw=academ-ic-0-20%7C438581&p=1179710&dv=c&gclid=EAIaIQobChMIj4PItoT-K3AIVSLbACh3Gigz4EAQYASABEgL2afD_BwE

53. Matthew 4:1-11

54. Boon, Brooke. Holy Yoga: Exercise. for the Christian Body and Soul. Published by FaithWords, 2007, ISBN-13: 978-0446699150

55. https://christiananswers.net/q-eden/rfsm-guru.html; Did Jesus ever travel to India? Accessed 07/03/2018 https://www.gotquestions.org/Jesus-India.html Accessed 07/03/2018

56. https://www.huffingtonpost.com/paul-davids/jesus-lost-years-may-fi-na_b_179513.html Accessed 07/12/2018

57. www.jesus-in-india-the-movie.com Accessed 06/12/2018

58. Deuteronomy 4:2 (ESV) Deuteronomy 12:32 (ESV), Revelation 22:18 (ESV),

Proverbs 30:5-6 (ESV), Ezekiel 44:10 (MSG)

59. Joyner, Rick. The Final Quest Trilogy. Morning Star Publications (October 18, 2016) ISBN-10: 1607086654; ISBN-13: 978-1607086659

60. https://www.yogaalliance.org/Portals/0/2016%20Yoga%20in%20America%20Study%20RESULTS.pdf (Accessed 08/06/2018)

61. Isaiah 5:20: Woe unto them that call evil good, and good evil; that put darkness for light, and light for darkness; that put bitter for sweet, and sweet for bitter!

62. Strong's Hebrew: https://biblehub.com/hebrew/5175.htm (Accessed 08/01/2018)

63. Luke 10:19

64. Revelation 12:9

65. https://www.ancient-origins.net/myths-legends/tracing-origins-serpent-cult-002393

66. Ancient Origins: https://www.ancient-origins.net/myths-legends/tracing-origins-serpent-cult-002393 (Accessed 08/02/2018)

67. John 1:1-6 (KJV).

68. John 1:4: In him was life; and the life was the light of men; John 1:5: And the light shineth in darkness; and the darkness comprehended it not; John 1:7: The same came for a witness, to bear witness of the Light, that all men through him might believe.

69. Revelation 13:1-18;1 John 2:18;2 Thessalonians 2:3-4; Revelation 12:9

70. 2 Thessalonians 2:4

71. Daniel 11:37-39

72. http://www.cogwriter.com/news/prophecy/are-some-hindus-inadvertantly-waiting-to-support-the-beast-and-false-prophet/ (Accessed 08/04/2018)

73. Hindu Prophecies: The Kalki Purarna http://ww-iii.tripod.com/hindu.htm (Accessed 08/06/2018)

74. http://www.jmanjackal.net/eng/engyoga.htm (Accessed 08/09/2018)

75. https://www.traditioninaction.org/History/G_029_Reiki_4.html (Accessed 05/08/2019)

76. Revelation 12:9, 12

77. Daniel chapter 4, verses 28-33

78. https://abcnews.go.com/Technology/story?id=98107&page=1 (Accessed 08/08/2018)

79. https://www.shalach.org/Antichrist/Who%20is%20the%20god%20of%20 forces.htm (Accessed 08/03/2018)

80. https://theslg.com/content/43-arthur-burk (Accessed 08/08/2018)

81. https://dougaddison.com/2018/07/how-to-minister-to-the-human-spirit-doug-addison-with-arthur-burk-episode-60/ (Accessed 08/08/2018)

82. Mishra, op.cit. https://bibleresources.org/yoga/(Accessed 08/08/2018)

83. Judaism and the Dangers of "Torah Yoga" http://shalach.org/TorahYoga/Yoga-Warning.htm (Accessed 08/04/2018)

84. (R.S Mishra's Yoga Sutras and Fundamentals of Yoga , J. Brennan's Astral Doorways, and H. Chaudhuri's Philosophy of Meditation are footnoted) https:// bibleresources.org/yoga/ (Accessed 08/01/2018)

85. K. Koch's Christian Counseling and Occultism https://bibleresources.org/ yoga/ (Accessed 08/01/2018) Christian Counseling and Occultism: A Complete Guidebook to Occult Oppression and Deliverance by Kurt E. Koch https://www.amazon.com/Christian-Counseling-Occultism-Oppression-Deliverance/dp/0825430100/ref=pd_lpo_sbs_14_t_1?_encoding=UTF8&psc=1&refRID=DM84F7EGC21Y9D5CQ681

86. https://bibleresources.org/yoga/ (Accessed 08/04/2018)

87. http://ericbarger.com/

88. The Prime-Time Occult Invasion, Published on 28 July 2018, https://olive-treeviews.org/radio-archives/ (Accessed 07/28/2018)

89. http://www.nydailynews.com/news/national/snake-house-horrors-idaho-family-driven-home-finding-thousands-serpents-article-1.128936 (Accessed 08/05/2018)

90. "It felt like it was Satan's lair." https://www.oregonlive.com/pacific-northwest-news/index.ssf/2011/06/family_flees_snake_house_it_felt_like_we_were_living_in_satans_lair.html (Accessed 08/05/2018)

91. Snakes in a Trailer https://www.animalplanet.com/tv-shows/fatal-attractions/full-episodes/snakes-in-a-trailer (Accessed 07/18/2018)

92. Genesis 20:3; Genesis 40:8; Daniel 1:17; Acts 2:17; Matthew 1:20-23; Matthew 2:13; Matthew 2:19; Joel 2:28; Daniel 7:1-3

93. Matthew 13:24-30; 36-43

94. [Quoting Sannyasin Arumugaswami. Apparently, the article quoting Arumugaswami first appeared in the Orlando Sentinel, May 14, 2006. See Laurette Willis, "Why a Christian ALTERNATIVE to Yoga?" Praise Moves. Online at: http://praisemoves.com/about-us/why-a-christian-alternative-to-yoga/.]

95. http://www.spiritual-research-network.com/f/SRN_0713July_WEB.pdf

96. [Danda, of the Dharma Yoga Ashram (Classical Yoga Hindu Academy, www. classicalyoga.org) located in Manahawkin, New Jersey, in a personal e-mail to the Lighthouse Trails Research Project. Used with permission.]

97. Awakening the Serpent Within? Yoga: an invitation to demonic possession. https://www.churchmilitant.com/news/article/awakening-the-serpent-within (Accessed 08/08/2018)

98. https://www.churchmilitant.com/news/article/awakening-the-serpent-within (Accessed 08/08/2018)

99. https://holyyoga.net/about/what-we-believe/ (Accessed 07/20/2018)

100. https://classroom.synonym.com/what-do-hindus-consider-sacred-12086225. html (Accessed 07/28/2018)

101. https://iskconeducationalservices.org/HoH/practice/503.htm (Accessed 07/29/2018)

102. 1 Corinthians 10:21 (NLT): You cannot drink from the cup of the Lord and from the cup of demons, too. You cannot eat at the Lord's Table and at the table of demons, too.

103. https://www.whatchristianswanttoknow.com/what-is-the-biblical-definition-of-holy/ (Accessed 08/09/18)

104. https://www.livestrong.com/article/395082-spiritual-meanings-of-yoga-postures/ (Accessed 08/03/2018)

105. (2 Chronicles 33:6 NKJV)

106. https://www.classicalyoga.org/spiritual-but-not-religious (Accessed 06/28/2018)

107. https://www.classicalyoga.org/real-hatha-yoga (Accessed 08/12/2018)

108. https://www.classicalyoga.org/what-is-real-yoga (Accessed 06/28/2018)

109. https://www.classicalyoga.org/spiritual-but-not-religious (Accessed 06/28/2018)

110. http://www.Yogapoint.com/info/article11.htm (Accessed 07/16/2018)

111. https://www.amazon.com/Yoga-Jesus-Understanding-Self-Realization-Fellowship/dp/0876125569/ref=tmm_pap_swatch_0?_encoding=UTF8&qid=&sr=&dpID=51M5r686kML&preST=_SY344_BO1,204,203,200_QL70_&dpSrc=detail

112. https://www.classicalyoga.org/what-is-real-yoga (Accessed 06/17/2018)

113. https://www.classicalyoga.org/spiritual-but-not-religious (Accessed 08/10/2018)

114. http://www.deephealing.eu/index.php/do-more/articles/13-testimony-of-deliverance-from-a-demon-of-yoga (Accessed 08/15/2018)

115. http://www.deephealing.eu/index.php/do-more/articles/13-testimony-of-deliverance-from-a-demon-of-yoga (Accessed 08/15/2018)

116. https://holyyoga.net/about/what-we-believe/ (Accessed 08/15/2018)

117. http://www.washingtontimes.com/news/2005/sep/22/20050922-114821-4035r/ (Accessed 08/15/2018)

118. https://edhird.com/2013/04/05/yoga-more-than-meets-the-eyes/ (Accessed 08/15/2018)

119. https://www.lighthousetrailsresearch.com/yoga.htm (Accessed 07/17/2018)

120. https://lifestylefrisco.com/frisco-holy-yoga/ (Accessed 07/14/2018)

121. Boon, Brooke. Holy Yoga: Exercise for the Christian Body and Soul (p. 16). FaithWords. Kindle Edition.

122. https://people.com/crime/children-of-god-survivor-on-child-sex-abuse-incest/ (Accessed 08/10/2018)

123. https://people.com/crime/children-of-god-survivor-on-child-sex-abuse-incest/ (Accessed 08/10/2018)

124. 124 https://www.theguardian.com/world/2017/mar/11/children-of-god-church-sex-cult-texas-mexico-fbi (Accessed 08/10/2018) Children of God cult was 'hell on earth' https://www.bbc.com/news/uk-scotland-44613932 (Accessed 08/10/2018) The hippie Christian cult that encouraged sex with children is still around today https://timeline.com/children-of-god-5245a45f6a2a (Accessed 08/10/2018) 'I grew up in a sex cult': surviving the Children of God abuse https://www.marieclaire.co.uk/opinion/children-of-god-586410 (Accessed 08/10/2018) Ex-Member of Free-Love Cult Details Child Sex Abuse, Incest: 'We Were Supposed to Be God's Whores' https://people.com/crime/children-of-god-survivor-on-child-sex-abuse-incest/ (Accessed 08/07/2018)

125. http://home.bt.com/news/on-this-day/march-26-1997-comet-hale-bopp-claims-the-lives-of-39-cult-members-as-it-flies-past-earth-11363970925759 (Accessed 08/03/2018) http://people.ucalgary.ca/~nurelweb/papers/irving/HGCC.html (Accessed 08/03/2018) http://www.cnn.com/US/9703/27/suicide/index.html (Accessed 08/03/2018) https://www.nytimes.com/1997/03/29/us/families-learning-of-39-cultists-who-died-willingly.html (Accessed 08/03/2018)

126. http://www.cnn.com/US/9703/27/suicide/index.html (Accessed 08/03/2018)

127. http://www.womenofgrace.com/blog/?p=13904 (Accessed 07/13/2018)

128. https://www.christianpost.com/news/holy-yoga-visits-seattle-area-50825/ (Accessed 06/08/2018)

129. https://www.todayschristianwoman.com/articles/2005/march/truth-about-yoga.html?&kwid=TCWppc&ad=85491001838&utm_source=google&gclid=EAIaIQobChMIy_6tjb2I3AIVULnACh2eKQN4EAMYASAAEgLV0_D_BwE

130. https://praisemoves.com/blog/12-reasons-why-yoga-is-not-good-for-christians/

131. http://www.piratechristian.com/museum-of-idolatry/2015/12/100-yoga-100-jesus-really-bad-math

132. https://www.nytimes.com/2012/02/28/health/nutrition/yoga-fans-sexual-flames-and-predictably-plenty-of- scandal.html?pagewanted=all (Accessed 07/03/2018)

133. https://www.amazon.com/gp/product/0830714499/ref=dbs_a_def_rwt_bibl_vppi_i19 (Accessed 08/21/2018)

134. https://www.truthbehindyoga.com/christian-yoga-and-yoga-for-exercise-only.html (Accessed 07/12/2018)

135. https://www.amazon.com/Fourth-Dimension-Dr-David-Yongghi-ebook/dp/B002LZUFNO/ref=sr_1_2?s=digital-text&ie=UTF8&qid=1534967922&sr=1-2&keywords=The+Fourth+Dimension+Cho (Accessed 08/21/2018)

136. https://whatsthematterwithyoga.wordpress.com (Accessed 07/15/2018)

137. http://www.christiananswersforthenewage.org/Articles_Yoga.html (Accessed 06/23/2018)

138. http://www.christiantruthcenter.com/untold-spiritual-truth-about-yoga/ (Accessed 06/27/2018)

139. http://sabc.cgld.org/ (Accessed 08/22/2018)

140. https://books.google.com/books?id=6epKAAAAQBAJ&pg=PT94&lpg=PT94&dq=ALFRED+CAWSTON+MISSIONARY&source=bl&ots=M-KU4iRExRD&sig=ZkyEHKshIG3JHV3w5WLADTpE2bk&hl=en&sa=X-&ved=2ahUKEwjryfOModHcAhVD_IMKHdEiAmQQ6AEwAXoECAcQA-Q#v=onepage&q=ALFRED%20CAWSTON%20MISSIONARY&f=false

141. https://books.google.com/books?id=6epKAAAAQBAJ&pg=PT94&lpg=PT94&dq=ALFRED+CAWSTON+MISSIONARY&source=bl&ots=M-KU4iRExRD&sig=ZkyEHKshIG3JHV3w5WLADTpE2bk&hl=en&sa=X-&ved=2ahUKEwjryfOModHcAhVD_IMKHdEiAmQQ6AEwAXoECAcQA-Q#v=onepage&q=ALFRED%20CAWSTON%20MISSIONARY&f=false

142. https://www.huffingtonpost.com/sura-flow/yoga-_b_2100857.html (Accessed 08/12/2018)

143. https://wildhunt.org/2012/02/update-yoga-scandals-and-sex-cults.html (Accessed 07/12/2018)

144. http://www.pasadenanow.com/main/pasadena-yoga-instructor-convict-ed-of-sexual-battery/#.W3H2Iy2ZOu4 (Accessed 08/12/2018)

145. https://theyogalunchbox.co.nz/a-compehrensive-list-of-yoga-scandals-involving-gurus-sex-and-other-inappropriate-behaviour/(Accessed 08/17/2018)

146. https://www.metro.us/lifestyle/twisted-relationships-inside-yoga-sex-scandals/tmWnbi---224ee5OU84HIM (Accessed 08/17/2018)

147. https://www.huffingtonpost.com/alanna-zabel/yoga-and-sex_b_4826422.html (Accessed 08/17/2018)

148. http://www.womenofgrace.com/blog/?p=12940 (Accessed 07/19/2018)

149. https://www.theguardian.com/lifeandstyle/2017/feb/18/bikram-hot-yoga-scandal-choudhury-what-he-wanted (Accessed 08/17/2018)

150. http://www.patheos.com/blogs/wildhunt/2012/02/update-yoga-scandals-and-sex-cults.html (Accessed 08/22/2018)

151. http://dailycaller.com/2018/06/14/yoga-in-metoo-era-and-started-as-sex-cult/ (Accessed 08/17/2018)

152. https://www.prnewswire.com/news-releases/yoga-massage-scandals-and-yoga-sex-scandals-a-response-from-yogi-dashama-142303705.html (Accessed 08/17/2018)

153. https://www.youtube.com/watch?v=SQAaq1rMdh4 (Accessed 08/21/2018)

154. http://anmolmehta.com/swami-nithyananda-sex-video-scandal-and-fraud/ (Accessed 08/17/2018)

155. http://yogadork.com/2014/12/16/satyananda-yoga-reeling-from-horrific-details-of-sex-abuse-rape-allegations-and-accountability/ (Accessed 08/17/2018)

156. https://www.thedailybeast.com/australias-underage-yoga-sex-cult-the-survivors-speak-out (Accessed 08/17/2018)

157. https://thedailybanter.com/issues/2013/03/29/sex-scandal-rocks-yoga-world/ (Accessed 08/17/2018)

158. https://www.healthista.com/sexual-abuse-in-yoga-the-secret-we-cant-ignore/ (Accessed 08/17/2018)

159. https://www.thedailybeast.com/the-mysterious-death-of-a-tantric-sex-guru (Accessed 08/17/2018)

160. https://www.nytimes.com/2012/02/28/health/nutrition/yoga-fans-sexual-flames-and-predictably-plenty-of-scandal.html?pagewanted=all (Accessed 07/03/2018)

161. http://huntergatherer.com/yoga-unmasked-as-pagan-sex-cult/ (Accessed 08/17/2018)

162. https://www.dallasnews.com/news/courts/2018/09/04/dallas-woman-claims-forced-faith-based-holy-yoga-reporting-sexual-harassment-class

163. https://www.yogapedia.com/definition/5190/dandasana (Accessed 08/09/2018)

164. https://www.yogapedia.com/definition/5190/dandasana (Accessed 08/09/2018)

165. https://www.livestrong.com/article/395082-spiritual-meanings-of-yoga-postures/ (Accessed 07/17/2018)

166. https://www.livestrong.com/article/395082-spiritual-meanings-of-yoga-postures/ (Accessed 07/17/2018)

167. http://www.spiritual-research-network.com/christianyoga.html (Accessed 07/17/2018)

168. Yoga more dangerous than previously thought, scientists say https://www.telegraph.co.uk/news/2017/06/28/yogamore-dangerous-previously-thought-scientists-say/ (Accessed 08/21/2018)

169. https://www.christianministriesintl.org/article/warning-christianity-and-yoga-do-not-mix/ (Accessed 08/21/2018)

170. https://www.charismanews.com/opinion/61880-ex-witch-reveals-connection-between-yoga-and-satan (Accessed 08/21/2018)

171. https://www.christiantoday.com/article/witch-turned-christian-says-there-is-a-connection-between-yoga-and-satan/103088.htm

172. https://www.truthbehindyoga.com/ Smith, Jessica, The Shattering – An Encounter with Truth (Accessed 08/23/2018)

173. https://www.truthbehindyoga.com/yoga.html (Accessed 08/23/2018)

174. Hunt, Dave and McMayhon, T.A., The Seduction of Christianity – Spiritual Discernment in the Last Days, p.54., Harvest House Publishers, Eugene, Oregon 97402

175. https://www.cai.org/testimonies/spiritual-deception-yoga (Accessed 07/03/2018)

176. https://christiannews.net/2018/08/22/concerns-raised-after-serita-jakes-posts-photos-of-yoga-session-at-the-potters-house-church/ (Accessed 08/27/2018)

177. http://www.foxnews.com/us/2018/01/29/americans-who-practice-yoga-contribute-to-white-supremacy-michigan-state-university-professor-claims.html (Accessed 08/28/2018) https://everydayfeminism.com/2016/05/yoga-cultural-appropriation/ (Accessed 08/27/2018)

178. https://www.lighthousetrailsresearch.com/blog/?p=18200 (Accessed 07/03/2018)

179. https://www.amazon.com/Larsons-New-Book-Cults-Larson/dp/0842328602

180. https://www.amazon.com/Larsons-World-Religions-Alternative-Spirituality/dp/084236417X

181. https://www.boblarson.org/bob-larson-warns-against-yoga/(Accessed 07/28/2018)

182. https://www.boblarson.org/bob-larson-warns-against-yoga/ (Accessed 07/28/2018)

183. https://www.boblarson.org/dont-yield-to-yoga-11-30-15/ (Accessed 07/19/2018)

184. www.DaveWilliams.com

185. O'Leary, UPWARD - Strategies for Success in Business, Life, and Relationships. https://davewilliams.com/product/upward-book/

186. [Dave Hunt cites Marilyn Ferguson in Yoga and the Body of Christ, Berean Call, 2007, p. 70]

187. http://indowave.tripod.com/HINDU.html (Accessed 08/25/2018)

188. 2 Corinthians 3:17

189. https://holyyoga.net/outreach/ (Accessed 06/15/2018)

190. https://www.collective-evolution.com/2017/02/07/christ-consciousness-you-have-the-same-capabilities-as-jesus-once-did/ (Accessed 07/23/2018)

191. http://www.christiandoctrine.com/christian-doctrine/anti-god-beliefs/1513-hinduism-satanic-to-its-core (Accessed 08/26/2018)

192. Dr. John Weldon authored or coauthored more than 80 books, holding a Ph.D. in comparative religion and a D. Min. with emphasis in contemporary religious movements. https://www.jashow.org/articles/yoga-the-occult/ (accessed 080/12/2018)

193. Rammurti S. Mishra, Yoga Sutras: The Textbook of Yoga Psychology, Garden City, NY: Anchor Books, 1973, pp. 132-37,295-399; Ernest Wood, Seven Schools of Yoga: An Introduction, Wheaton, IL: Theosophical Publishing House, 1973, pp. 112-13; R. S. Mishra, Fundamentals of Yoga, Garden City, NY: Anchor, 1974, pp. 2-3, chs. 17-19, 26- 27; J. H. Brennan, Astral Doorways, New York: Samuel Weiser, 1972, pp. 29, 98; Haridas Chaudhuri, Philosophy of Meditation, New York: Philosophical Library, 1974, pp. 50-51.

194. https://www.dictionary.com/browse/subterfuge?s=t (Accessed 08/28/2018)

195. https://www.cai.org/testimonies/spiritual-deception-yoga (Accessed 07/02/2018)

196. Caryl Matrisciana, God's of the New Age, Harvest House Publishers, 1985

cited http://truthwatchers.com/yoga-dangers-spiritual-deception/ (Accessed 08/27/2018)

197. 197http://religionandamericanlaw.blogspot.com/2013/11/is-yoga-religious. html (Accessed 08/28/2018)

198. Caryl Matrisciana, God's of the New Age, Harvest House Publishers, 1985, p. 145

199. Paul, Pamela, Time magazine, Oct 15, 2007, p. 71

200. Paul, Pamela, Time magazine, Oct 15, 2007, p. 71

201. http://truthwatchers.com/yoga-dangers-spiritual-deception/ (Accessed 08/26/2018)

202. These statistics are based on a study of the TM (Transcendental Meditation) form of yoga, and was pursued by the German Government youth department (Ministry of Youth, Family and Health), which was verified by the nations Supreme Courts after careful review. http://truthwatchers.com/yoga-dangers-spiritual-deception/ (Accessed 08/26/2018)

203. http://truthwatchers.com/yoga-dangers-spiritual-deception/

204. Wood, Ernest, Seven Schools of Yoga, 1976, p. 12, 78, 79

205. https://www.yogajournal.com/lifestyle/study-finds-yoga-injuries-are-on-the-rise-plus-4-ways-to-avoid-them (Accessed 08/27/2018)

206. Broad, New York Times, How Yoga can Wreck your Body https://www.nytimes.com/2012/01/08/magazine/how-yoga-can-wreck-your-body.html (Accessed 08/27/2018)

207. https://www.sciencedaily.com/releases/2017/06/170627105433.htm (Accessed 08/27/2018)

208. http://www.abc.net.au/news/2018-04-10/yoga-injuries-on-the-rise/9634154 (Accessed 08/27/2018)

209. https://bottomlineinc.com/life/yoga/yoga-can-be-dangerous (Accessed 08/27/2018)

210. https://eluxemagazine.com/beauty/dangers-of-yoga-postures/ (Accessed 08/27/2018)

211. https://www.christianitytoday.com/women-leaders/2012/june/discernment-as-way-of-life.html (Accessed 08/28/2018)

212. https://www.goodreads.com/author/quotes/145073.J_Wilbur_Chapman (Accessed 05/23/2018)

213. https://www.jpost.com/Opinion/Why-is-Adolf-Hitler-popular-in-India-376622 (Accessed 08/28/2018)

214. Tieke, Mathias. Yoga im Nationalsozialismus: Konzepte, Kontraste, Konsequenzen Taschenbuch Steve-Holger Ludwig; Auflage: Überarbeitete Nachauflage. September 2011. You may also be interested in reading about the Nazi death marches. Blatman, Daniel. The Death Marches: The Final Phase of Nazi Genocide. Belknap Press; Translation edition: December 23, 2010

215. Speech 26 June 1934; from Norman H. Baynes, ed. (1969). The Speeches of Adolf Hitler: April 1922-August 1939. 1. New York: Howard Fertig. p. 385.

216. https://en.wikipedia.org/wiki/Positive_Christianity (Accessed 09/02/2018) And "The National Socialist State professes its allegiance to positive Christianity." [Speech 26 June 1934; from Norman H. Baynes, ed. (1969). The Speeches of Adolf Hitler: April 1922-August 1939. 1. New York: Howard Fertig. p. 385.]

217. Shirer, William L. (1960). The Rise and Fall of the Third Reich. London: Secker & Warburg. pp. 238–39.

218. https://yeahdave.com/yoga-and-the-nazis/ (Accessed 09/11/2018)

219. https://fineartamerica.com/shop/yoga+mats/adolf+hitler (accessed 09/10/2018)

220. https://www.yogajournal.com/.amp/lifestyle/yoga-on-the-white-house-lawn (Accessed 09/03/2018)

221. http://yogadork.com/2018/02/15/obamas-presidential-center-first-to-include-a-yoga-room/ (Accessed 09/12/2018)

222. https://www.indiatimes.com/news/india/a-french-hindu-writer-believed-that-hitler-was-an-avatar-of-lord-vishnu-here-s-her-story-327573.html (Accessed 08/29/2018)

223. https://www.amazon.com/Kundalini-Collective-Awakening-Krishan-Khalsa/dp/0473011964

224. 224 https://www.britannica.com/biography/Dietrich-Bonhoeffer (Accessed 09/03/2018) and https://en.wikipedia.org/wiki/Dietrich_Bonhoeffer / (Accessed 09/03/2018)

225. https://www.ibtimes.com/nazi-germanys-fascination-ancient-india-case-heinrich-himmler-214364 (Accessed 09/03/2018)

226. https://www.telegraph.co.uk/history/world-war-two/9098525/Nazi-leader-Heinrich-Himmler-a-fan-of-yoga.html (Accessed 09/05/2018)Also: http://yogadork.com/2012/02/21/apparently-the-third-reich-had-a-fascination-with-yog a-in-nazi-germany/ (Accessed 08/28/2018)

227. https://encyclopedia.ushmm.org/content/en/article/ghettos (Accessed 09/04/2018)

228. The SS was the organization most responsible for the genocidal killing of an

283

estimated 5.5 to 6 million Jews and millions of other victims in the Holocaust. https://en.wikipedia.org/wiki/Schutzstaffel Accessed 05/03/2019

229. http://www.dailymail.co.uk/news/article-2104365/How-SS-recommended-yoga-death-camp-guards-good-way-stress.html (Accessed 09/04/2018)

230. https://www.consumerreports.org/cro/2014/02/dangers-of-hot-yoga/index.htm (Accessed 09/12/2018)

231. Romans 12:3 MSG

232. https://www.theatlantic.com/national/archive/2012/01/cocktail-crossfire-yoga-crock/316346/ (Accessed 09/04/2018)

233. https://www.bmj.com/content/bmj/1/5801/685.2.full.pdf (Retrieved 08/27/18) (Accessed 08/24/2018)

234. http://www.deephealing.eu/index.php/do-more/articles/13-testimony-of-deliverance-from-a-demon-of-yoga (Accessed 09/05/2018)

235. http://www.theothersideofdarkness.com

236. Matthew 24:21(NKJV) : For then there will be great tribulation, such as has not been since the beginning of the world until this time, no, nor ever shall be.

237. Revelation 13:2 (NKJV): The dragon gave him his power, his throne, and great authority.

238. Revelation 13:5

239. Kah, Gary. The New World Religion, p. 246

240. Brooke, Tal. The Great Lie. SCP Journal 29:2-29:3, p. 11 /

241. Hislop, Alexander. The Two Babylons. 4th Edition Chick Pub (1998)

242. https://www.psychologytoday.com/us/blog/urban-survival/201506/why-does-anyone-do-yoga-anyway

243. Mukerji, Swamie A.P., Yoga Lessons for Developing Spiritual Consciousness, 2007, Miller Press

244. https://www.dictionary.com/browse/triumvirate?s=t

245. Deuteronomy 6:4

246. http://www.oxfordscholarship.com/mobile/view/10.1093/0199284598.001.0001/acprof-9780199284597-chapter-7 (Accessed/Retrieved 06/26/2018)

247. https://strangenotions.com/three-false-christs-the-myth-the-mortal-and-the-guru/ (Accessed/Retrieved 06/09/2018)

248. http://www.harekrishnatemple.com/jesusguru.html (Accessed/Retrieved 08/02/2018)

249. https://www.cai.org/files/theme-sheets/en/dw2/SW2030AU%20-%20Counterfeit%20Spirituality.PDF

250. https://en.wikipedia.org/wiki/Paramahansa_Yogananda (Accessed 08/22/2018)

251. https://www.collective-evolution.com/2017/02/07/christ-consciousness-you-have-the-same-capabilities-as-jesus-once-did/ (Accessed 07/17/2018)

252. https://www.youtube.com/watch?v=ppk-iFMrmV4 (Accessed 09/15/2018)

253. https://en.wikipedia.org/wiki/Brahma (Accessed 09/15/2018)

254. https://www.ancient.eu/Brahma/ (Accessed 09/16/2018)

255. http://www.bbc.co.uk/religion/religions/hinduism/deities/brahma.shtml (Accessed 09/15/2018)

256. http://www.bbc.co.uk/religion/religions/hinduism/deities/vishnu.shtml (Accessed 09/16/2018)

257. https://www.britannica.com/topic/Vishnu (Accessed 09/16/2018)

258. https://www.ancient.eu/shiva/ (Accessed 09/16/2018)

259. Shiva Lingam - How the Worship of a Penis started in Hinduism http://www.jaisiyaram.com/blog/religion/18894-shiva-lingam-how-the-worship-of-a-penis-started-in-hinduism-17-feb-15.html (Accessed 09/12/2018)

260. 1 Corinthians 10:20-21

261. What is an Asherah pole? https://www.gotquestions.org/Asherah-pole.html For further study of Asherah: https://www.thattheworldmayknow.com/fertility-cults-of-canaan http://wideawakechristian.blogspot.com/2014/10/the-terrifying-return-of-asherah.html?m=1 https://www.google.com/amp/s/www.gotquestions.org/amp/who-Asherah.html http://www.pursuegod.org/idolatry-in-israel-asherah/

262. https://en.wikiquote.org/wiki/Tertullian

263. I Corinthians 4:14

264. https://www.dallasnews.com/news/courts/2018/09/04/dallas-woman-claims-forced-faith-based-holy-yoga-reporting-sexual-harassment-class (Accessed 10/18/2018)

265. Copy of Complaint can be found here: https://www.scribd.com/document/387764413/Galvis-v-Holy-Yoga-NDTX-318-Cv-02081 (Accessed 10/18/2018)

266. https://www.pacermonitor.com/public/case/25309956/Galvis_v_Holy_Yoga_Foundation_et_al

267. https://www.kqed.org/news/11690316/metoo-unmasks-the-open-secret-of-

sexual-abuse-in-yoga (Accessed 10/18/2018)

268. 1 Corinthians 12:28; Ephesians 4:11

269. 2 Timothy 4:3 (AMP)

270. 2 Peter 2:1 (AMP)2 Peter 2:12 (AMP), 2 Peter 2:17 (AMP), 2 Peter 2:18-19 (NKJV).

271. 1 John 4:1 (AMP)

272. https://www.azquotes.com/quote/718769 (Accessed 10/03/2018)

273. After Hitler and his wife committed suicide, Goebbels served as chancellor of Germany for one day before he and his wife, Magda, poisoned their six children and took their own lives. https://www.historians.org/about-aha-and-member-ship/aha-history-and-archives/gi-roundtable-series/pamphlets/em-2-what-is-propaganda-(1944)/what-are-the-tools-of-propaganda (Accessed 10/03/2018)

274. https://www.historians.org/about-aha-and-membership/aha-history-and-ar-chives/gi-roundtable-series/pamphlets/em-2-what-is-propaganda-(1944)/what-are-the-tools-of-propaganda (Accessed 09/18/2018)

275. https://www.physics.smu.edu/pseudo/Propaganda/goebbels.html (Accessed 10/02/2018) Goebbels' Principles of Propaganda, Leonard W. Doob, Public Opinion Quarterly, Fall 1950 pp. 419-442Propagation and Persuasion; Jowett & O'Donnell, https://www.amazon.com/Propaganda-Persuasion-Garth-S-Jowett/dp/1412977827

276. 7 Sure-Fire Ways to Recognize False Teachers by John UpChurch https://www.crosswalk.com/blogs/christian-trends/7-sure-fire-ways-to-recognize-false-teachers.html (Accessed 10/02/2018)

277. http://www.bbc.com/future/story/20161026-how-liars-create-the-illu-sion-of-truth?ocid=fbfut (Accessed 09/18/2018)

278. https://www.wired.com/2017/02/dont-believe-lies-just-people-repeat/ (Accessed 09/25/2018)

279. https://iblp.org/questions/what-are-common-characteristics-teachers (Accessed 10/17/2018)

280. Galatians 6:7

281. The Yoga System Of Patañjali, translated from the original Sanskrit by James Haughton Woods, Professor of Philosophy at Harvard University, Cambridge, Massachusetts, University Press 1914.

282. https://www.crosswalk.com/faith/spiritual-life/is-it-okay-for-christians-to-practice-yoga.html (Accessed 10/27/2018)

283. http://seekgodstruth.com/sotdangersofyoga.html (Accessed 10/27/2018)

284. Excerpts from Bill Wong's article, The Dangers of Yoga http://seekgodstruth. com/sotdangersofyoga.html (Accessed 10/27/2018)

285. Jeremiah 3:20; Isaiah 1:21; 57:8; Ezekiel 16:30

286. Deuteronomy 32:17 NLT: They offered sacrifices to demons, which are not God, to gods they had not known before, to new gods only recently arrived, to gods their ancestors had never feared. 1 Corinthians 10:19-21 NLT:...I am saying that these sacrifices are offered to demons, not to God. And I don't want you to participate with demons. 21 You cannot drink from the cup of the Lord and from the cup of demons, too. You cannot eat at the Lord's Table and at the table of demons, too.

287. Revelation 9:20 NLT: But the people who did not die in these plagues still refused to repent of their evil deeds and turn to God. They continued to worship demons and idols made of gold, silver, bronze, stone, and wood—idols that can neither see nor hear nor walk!

288. Revelation 18:2 NLT: He gave a mighty shout: "Babylon is fallen—that great city is fallen! She has become a home for demons. She is a hideout for every foul spirit, a hideout for every foul vulture and every foul and dreadful animal.

289. Deuteronomy 11:28 NKJV

290. 2 Corinthians 11:4

291. https://www.dailywire.com/news/26640/walsh-matt-walsh (Accessed 11/25/2018)

292. 2 Timothy 4:3

293. https://olivetreeviews.org/radio-archives/warning-when-the-east-seduces-the-church/ (Accessed 12/04/2018)

294. www.thetruthbehindyoga.com (Accessed 11/25/2018)

295. https://www.amazon.com/Shattering-Encounter-Truth-Jessica-Smith/ dp/0942507193/ref=sr_1_1?s=books&ie=UTF8&qid=1542384951&s- r=1-1&keywords=the+shattering+jessica+smith

296. http://christinprophecy.org/sermons/matrisciana-on-christian-yoga/ (Accessed 11/25/2018)

297. https://friendlyatheist.patheos.com/2018/11/15/megachurch-pastor-john-lin- dell-yoga-is-evil-because-hinduism-is-demonic/

298. https://www.jonasclark.com/counterfeit-holyspirit-yoga-kundali- ni-demons/?start=1

299. https://www.themindfulword.org/2017/kundalini-awakening-energetic-trans- formation/ (Accessed 11/25/2018)

300. https://med.virginia.edu/perceptual-studies/wp-content/uploads/

sites/267/2015/11/NDE24.pdf

301. Ben Snyder , The Ministry of Dean Hochstetler 1974-2005, ISBN: 978-1-387-89571-7, pp 126-127

302. Ben Snyder , The Ministry of Dean Hochstetler 1974-2005, ISBN: 978-1-387-89571-7, p127

303. https://www.wikihow.com/Awaken-the-Kundalini (Accessed 12/04/2018)

304. https://theyogalunchbox.co.nz/kundalini-awakenings-symptoms-process-benefits-support-help/

305. https://www.jesus-is-lord.com/contemplative5.htm (Accessed 11/24/2018)

306. https://www.jonasclark.com/counterfeit-holyspirit-yoga-kundalini-demons/ (Accessed 10/30/2018)

307. http://kundalinipeak.com/myresources/ebooks/KundaliniEnergy_YogasOccultPhenomenaintheChurch.pdf (Accessed 12/04/2018)

308. https://www.newswithviews.com/West/marsha61.htm (Accessed 12/07/2018)

309. http://kundalinipeak.com/myresources/ebooks/KundaliniEnergy_YogasOccultPhenomenaintheChurch.pdf (Accessed 12/04/2018)

310. Chris Lawson asks, "Does Your Pastor Know That Yoga And Christianity Are Not Compatible?" https://www.lighthousetrailsresearch.com/blog/?p=22967 (Accessed 12/04/2018)

311. Tex Marrs, Mystery Mark of the New Age: Satan's Designs for World Domination, Crossway Books, Page 39

312. John 10:10; 2 John 1:8-11; John 8:32

313. https://www.athenaeum.edu/pdf/ChristianityHinduism.pdf (Accessed 11/24/2018)

314. Pittman, Nancy Chandler (2003) Christian Wicca: The Trinitarian Tradition 1st Books Library, ISBN 1-4107-5347-6

315. St Clair, Adelina. The Path of a Christian Witch. Woodbury MN: Llewellyn Publications. ISBN 978-0-7387-2641-0

316. Yamamori,Tetsunao. Christopaganism or Indigenous Christianity .William Carey Library Publishers McColman, Carl. Embracing Jesus and the Goddess: A Radical Call for Spiritual Sanity (2001). Gloucester, MA: Fair Winds PressHigginbotham, Joyce & River. ChristoPaganism: An Inclusive Path (2009), Woodbury MN: Llewellyn Publications. ISBN 978-0-7387-1467-7

317. https://www.christianitytoday.com/biblestudies/articles/theology/071205.html (Accessed 12/06/2018)

318. http://donlehmanjr.com/Articles/Yoga%203.htm (Accessed 12/07/2018)

319. https://www.thesaurus.com/browse/shaman (Accessed 11/24/2018)

320. Video: The Shamanic Roots of Yoga https://www.youtube.com/watch?v=b9K-T7rVgynk (Accessed 12/03/2018)

321. Yoga as a Shamanic Practice https://upliftconnect.com/yoga-as-shamanic-practice/ (Accessed 12/07/2018)

322. The Yoga System Of Patañjali, translated from the original Sanskrit by James Haughton Woods, Professor of Philosophy at Harvard University, CAMBRIDGE, MASSACHUSETTS, University Press 1914.

323. Yoga Through Christ: Via the Eight Limbs of Yoga by Sally Bassett Ph.D https://www.amazon.com/Yoga-Through-Christ-Eight-Limbs-ebook/dp/B06W2HHSGY (Accessed 11/24/2018)

324. http://www.christianspracticingyoga.com/the-eight-limbs-of-yoga/ (Accessed 12/07/2018)

325. https://www.shamanicyoga108.com/shamanic-yoga-what-is-it/ (Accessed 12/05/2018)

326. 2 Timothy 3:16

327. John 1:1-4; 10-13; Colossians 1:16-18

328. Acts 10:38

329. John 14:6-7 (NKJV):"

330. John 19:30

331. 1 Corinthians 15:3-4 (NKJV)s

332. John 3:2-7 (NKJV)

333. Acts 5:31; Acts 26:18; Ephesians 1:7; Colossians 1:14

334. 2 Peter 1:4

335. 1 Corinthians 2:13; John 16:13

336. Matthew 6:24 (NKJV)

337. Yoga and Christianity: Are They Compatible? – A Biblical Worldview Perspective Michael Gleghorn takes a hard look at yoga to determine if the practice is compatible with Christian living. After examining the spiritual underpinnings of yoga and the relationship of the physical aspects to the spiritual teaching, he concludes that Christians seeking physical exercise would be wise to consider techniques other than yoga. https://probe.org/yoga-and-christianity-are-they-compatible/ (Accessed 12/06/2018)

338. The Shattering – An Encounter With Truth by Jessica Smith http://deeper-

revelationbooks.org/cms/index.php?mact=Products,cntnt01,details,0&cntnt-01productid=137&cntnt01returnid=120 Luke 15:10, Matthew 10:32, Luke 12:8

339. Luke 15:10

340. Matthew 10:32: "Therefore whoever confesses Me before men, him I will also confess before My Father who is in heaven. Luke 12:8 "Also I say to you, whoever confesses Me before men, him the Son of Man also will confess before the angels of God.

341. Matthew 28:20

ADDITIONAL RESOURCES THAT MAY INTEREST YOU

Are There Many Paths to God? By Lee Strobel
https://www.christianitytoday.com/biblestudies/articles/theology/071205.html

700 Club Interview with former Yoga Instructor
http://www1.cbn.com/700club/should-christians-do-yoga

Dr. David Reagan interview: Yoga
https://www.youtube.com/watch?v=JKHwwsixFWw

Yoga and Your Christian Walk
http://www.doormousehouse.com/2013/10/yoga-your-christian-walk-never-twain.html

Christian Yoga? Take a Pass on Yoga
https://praisemoves.com/articles/christian-yoga/

Yoga Uncoiled
https://youtu.be/A5DUqQq3dJ8

From New Age To Jesus – Steven Bancarz Testimony
https://www.youtube.com/watch?v=cMu5F2icsT8

"No Christian Should Ever Do Yoga" – Former Yoga Instructor
https://www.youtube.com/watch?v=nZsqcKLOCDk

Yoga and the Occult: Ex Witch Tells All
https://www.youtube.com/watch?v=uoxs8ixsmrk

The Other Side of Darkness
http://www.theothersideofdarkness.com/

Is it Wrong for a Christian to do Yoga?
https://www.youtube.com/watch?v=NNhNfsWU-U8

Origins of Yoga
http://donlehmanjr.com/Articles/Yoga%203.htm

Ancient Wisdom on a New Path: Where Yoga and Shamanism Meet
https://kripalu.org/resources/ancient-wisdom-new-path-where-yoga-and-shamanism-meet

Adverse Events Associated with Yoga: A Systematic Review of Published Case Reports and Case Series
https://www.ncbi.nlm.nih.gov/pmc/articles/PMC3797727/

Yoga more dangerous than previously thought, scientists say
https://www.telegraph.co.uk/.../yogamore-dangerous-previously-thought-scientists-say/

My Yoga is Easy: Hinduization of Christianity
"There is no Hinduism without Yoga and there is no Yoga without Hinduism."
http://midwestoutreach.org/2007/10/04/my-yoga-is-easy-hinduization-of-christianity/

Serious Allegations
http://www.espn.com/espnw/culture/feature/article/23539292/after-serious-allegations-founder-bikram-yoga-practitioners-crossroads

Entertaining Spirits Unaware: The End-Time Occult Invasion by Eric Barger and David Benoit
http://ericbarger.com/enterspirits.htm

"Christians" Who Defend the Occult
http://ericbarger.com/christians.occult.htm

The Religious Nature of Yoga by Apologetics Resource Center
https://arcapologetics.org/culture/the-religious-nature-of-yoga/

What the Bible Says about Yoga? Is there such a thing as Christian Yoga?
By Sherif Michael
https://bibleresources.org/yoga/

Jessica Smith Testimony – Set free from Yoga demons!
https://www.youtube.com/watch?v=kYTp2kItbls
https://www.youtube.com/watch?v=xZ2o8vZZWr8

Freedom from demons of New Age, Yoga, and Occult
https://www.youtube.com/watch?v=cyOLiWivyew

Never ever do YOGA! The Danger of Yoga
https://www.youtube.com/watch?v=7Q1fpaxo0ts

Yoga teacher delivered of demons! Powerful testimony
https://www.youtube.com/watch?v=qneQpVzsVK0

Five Reasons why I No Longer Do Yoga
http://www.wholyfit.com/wp-content/uploads/2012/01/mike-Shreve.pdf

Yoga Dangers
https://www.yogadangers.com/christianity-and-yoga/christian-yoga/

Yoga: the Dangers of Spiritual Deception
http://truthwatchers.com/yoga-dangers-spiritual-deception/

What is Holy Yoga?
https://www.gotquestions.org/holy-yoga.html

Christian yoga: A Product of Hinduism and the New Age Movement by Injib Kim
https://digitalcommons.liberty.edu/cgi/viewcontent.cgi?article=1113&context=masters

Yoga: Can a Pagan Practice be "Christianized?" – Yoga
https://echristian.wordpress.com/tag/yoga/

Why Yoga Should Be Compared To Drinking Bleach
https://whygodreallyexists.com/archives/your-inner-god-why-yoga-should-be-compared-to-drinking-bleach

Why I Quit My Yoga Class
http://www.beginnerbeans.com/2013/07/should-christians-practice-yoga.html?m=1

The Perils of Poses: Yoga-related injuries
https://lermagazine.com/cover_story/the-perils-of-poses-yoga-related-injuries

How Yoga Can Wreck Your Body
https://www.nytimes.com/2012/01/08/magazine/how-yoga-can-wreck-your-body.html

Yoga: The Dangers of Spiritual Deception
http://truthwatchers.com/yoga-dangers-spiritual-deception/

Yoga is a Dangerous Spiritual Discipline
https://teachinghumblehearts.com/en/yoga-dangerous-spiritual-discipline/

"Yoga is the union of the individual psyche with the transcendental Self."
Yoga-Yajnavadka 1.44 quoted in "The Yoga Tradition. Its History, Literature, Philosophy and Practice" by Georg Feuerstein,
PH.D. Hohm Press, Prescott, Arizona, 1998, xviii

SUGGESTED BOOKS:
Entertaining Spirits Unaware
by Eric Barger and David Benoit

Psychic Forces and Occult Shock
by Clifford Wilson and John Weldon, Global Publishing 1987

Christian Counseling and Occultism: A Complete Guidebook to
Occult Oppression and Deliverance by Kurt E. Koch, Kregel
Publications; 21st edition edition,1972

Final Quest by Rick Joyner, Morningstar Publications, 2006

Biblical Demonology: A Study of Spiritual Forces at Work Today
by Merrill F. Unger, Kregel Publications, 2011

Like Lambs to the Slaughter by Johanna Michaelsen, Harvest
House Publishers, 1989

The Kingdom of the Cults (Revised Ed.); by Walter Martin, Ravi
K. Zacharias, Jill Martin Rische, Kevin Rische, 2003, Edi-
tion1672, Walter Ralston Martin Publishing

The Second Coming of the New Age: The Hidden Dangers
of Alternative Spirituality in Contemporary America and Its
Churches by Josh Peck and Steven Bancarz, Defender Publishing, 2018

The Shattering : An Encounter With Truth, Jessica Smith, Deeper Revelation Books, 2015

Knowing the Facts about Yoga, John Ankerberg and John Weldon, ATRI Publishing, 2012

Out of India, Caryl Matrisciana, Lighthouse Trails Publishing, 2017

Yoga and the Body of Christ: What Position Should Christians Hold? D. Hunt, The Berean Call, 2007

Seven Reasons I No Longer Practice Hatha Yoga, Mike Shreve, Deeper Revelation Books, 2015

The Highest Adventure Encountering God by Mike Shreve, Deeper Revelation Books, 2011

In Search of the True Light by Mike Shreve, Deeper Revelation Books; 2nd edition, 2007

Death of a Guru: A Remarkable True Story of one Man's Search for Truth by Rabi R. Maharaj, Harvest House Publishers, 1984

Larson's Book of World Religions and Alternative Spirituality by Bob Larson, Tyndale House Publishers, Inc., 2004

Powerful Prayers for Supernatural Results: How to Pray as Moses, Elijah, Hannah, and Other Biblical Heroes Did by Mike Shreve, Charisma House Publishers, 2014

Larson's Book of Cults (Tyndale House Publishers, Wheaton, Ill, 1982) ISBN 0-8423-2104-7

Larson's Book of Family Issues (Tyndale, 1986) ISBN 0-8423-2459-3

Strange Cults in America by Bob Larson (Tyndale, 1986) ISBN 0-8423-6675-X

Straight Answers on the New Age by Bob Larson (Thomas Nelson, 1989) ISBN 0-8407-3032-2

Tough Talk About Tough Issues by Bob Larson (Tyndale, 1989) ISBN 0-8423-7297-0

Larson's New Book of Cults (Tyndale, 1989) ISBN 0-8423-2860-2

Larson's Book of Spiritual Warfare (Nelson, 1999) ISBN 0-7852-6985-1

The Second Coming of the New Age by Steven Bancarz and Josh Peck, Defender Publishing, 2018

For a clear, concise understanding of Biblical Prophecies concerning the last days, the author urges you to get a copy of his Charisma Frontline book, *Hope in the Last Days*, available at Amazon, Barnes and Noble, Christian Book Distributors, Charisma, Walmart.com, and wherever books are sold.

Also available at www.DaveWilliams.com

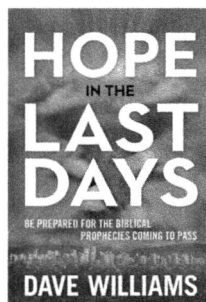